Hanif Kureishi's
The Buddha of Suburbia

CONTINUUM CONTEMPORARIES

Also available in this series

Forthcoming in this series:

· **HANIF KUREISHI'S**

The
Buddha
of
Suburbia

A READER'S GUIDE

NAHEM YOUSAF

CONTINUUM | NEW YORK | LONDON

2002

The Continuum International Publishing Group Inc
370 Lexington Avenue, New York, NY 10017

The Continuum International Publishing Group Ltd
The Tower Building, 11 York Road, London SE1 7NX

www.continuumbooks.com

Copyright © 2002 by Nahem Yousaf

Printed in the United States of America

Library of Congress Cataloging-in-Publication Data

Yousaf, Nahem.
    Hanif Kureishi's The buddha of suburbia : a reader's guide / Nahem
Yousaf.
        p. cm.—(Continuum contemporaries)
Includes bibliographical references.
    ISBN 0-8264-5324-4 (pbk. : alk. paper)
    1. Kureishi, Hanif. Buddha of suburbia. 2. London (England)—In
literature. 3. Fathers and sons in literature. 4. East Indians in
literature. I. Title. II. Series.
PR6061.U68 B8 2002
823'.92—dc21
                            2002000992

Contents

·**1**

The Novelist

The protagonist of *The Buddha of Suburbia*, Karim Amir, describes himself as a "funny kind of Englishman, a new breed as it were, having emerged from two old histories" (3) and it is this historicized tension between the history of the colonizer and the colonized that characterizes Hanif Kureishi the author. Born in 1954 to an English mother and an Asian father, Kureishi's creative output investigates and explores what it means to hold a position in society, indeed, a position within identity that is predicated on plurality rather than singularity. In his essay "The Rainbow Sign" he describes the relationship and its significance in succinct terms:

The two countries, Britain and Pakistan, have been part of each other for years, usually to the advantage of Britain. They cannot now be wrenched apart, even if that were desirable. Their futures will be intermixed. What that intermix means, its moral quality, whether it is violently resisted by ignorant whites and characterized by inequality and injustice, or understood, accepted and humanized, is for all of us to decide.

Kureishi has said on many occasions that he wanted to be a writer and was sufficiently disciplined as a school child to write novels and short stories in his evenings at home. But his early efforts, like those of his father, were destined to remain unpublished. In fact it wasn't until he was a student at a university in London that he found some publishing success writing for pornographic magazines under such pseudonyms like Antonia French and Karim, the latter the name he goes on to choose for the protagonist of his first novel. His breakthrough came in 1980 when his plays were accepted: two for the stage, *The King and Me* and *The Mother Country*, and *You Can't Go Home* for BBC radio. He continued to write for the stage, winning the George Devine award in 1981 and becoming the Royal Court's Writer-in-Residence in the same year. In the following year his play, *Borderline*, was a winner in Thames Television's Bursary scheme and he adapted Kafka's *The Trial* for BBC radio. However, widespread success didn't come until 1985 when Kureishi scripted *My Beautiful Laundrette*, the screenplay for which he was nominated for an Academy Award. His next film, *Sammy and Rosie Get Laid*, received a lukewarm reception from critics and viewing audiences alike. However, it was money earned from this film that allowed him the security to take a two-year break in which he could concentrate on writing what would become *The Buddha of Suburbia*. The idea for the novel had been around since 1987 when Kureishi published a version of the first chapter as a short story in *Harper's* magazine. This is unsurprising since Kureishi, as he says below, often writes and rewrites stories and returns to characters until he is satisfied that he has exhausted what he wants to say about them and their contexts.

AN INTERVIEW WITH HANIF KUREISHI

Your interests are eclectic: you have cited African American and Russian novelists, short story writers like Maupassant, and your contemporaries, like Rushdie. How do you find your own voice as a writer?[1]

I do think I have my own voice but I can only tell you that I am naturally influenced by everything I hear and read. I guess you might say that is the postmodern condition. There is inevitably such a range of influences and associations, as there is in Salman Rushdie's work too, for example.

Is it true that Rushdie encouraged you into writing novels?

He did in that he knew the screenplays but felt that the novel was the thing to work on in a sustained way and he told me I should get writing one! I was a bit stung to begin with but I remember it fondly. I was always just about to start on a novel and then I did, *The Buddha of Suburbia.*

*Could you cast your mind back to the publication of **Buddha**. Were you surprised by its overwhelming success? And how do you feel about its endurance as a classic of contemporary fiction?*

I am pleased it has held up. I wanted to write a book that people would want to read ten years later. But I am also pleased that works like *Buddha* and *My Beautiful Laundrette* helped to open the publishers' doors for other writers because you forget that when I started writing people asked "Why are you writing about *Asians?* Who is interested in minorities?" You can't believe it now but when *My Beautiful Laundrette* came out it proved it was possible to make a film about Asian people that other people wanted to see: people went to see it and it was popular and made money. It is hard to get into that position in the first place. I remember applying for a bursary and being told, "You are going to be in a writers' ghetto if you write about Asian people. Don't do that." It was really insulting and offensive. So it is important to me, and I think to others who get through to publishers now. A novel like Zadie Smith's *White*

Teeth can be a huge hit now whereas we used to be described as "Commonwealth Literature." To be located in that way is a form of ghettoisation.

You have managed to deconstruct that ghettoisation in innovative ways. For example, Jay, the protagonist of Intimacy, doesn't wear his ethnicity on his sleeve so I think the reader is quite surprised to discover some way in to the book that he is of mixed heritage.

You expect to recognise ethnicity but no-one says that a white character is white. It can unsettle the reader.

There used to be the expectation that black and Asian writers would write about racism and victim status, what writer Barbara Burford called "a little black pain undressed."[2]

There are always expectations. Asian people aren't "Asian" for me any more than white people are "white" for white people. They are just people. I was writing about my father not "an Asian man." You couldn't get too caught up in issues of representation and continue to write.

But the burden of representation did fall on you. There were those who expected you to smash stereotypes and create only positive representations.

Yes, I was in New York when *My Beautiful Laundrette* came out and people demonstrated, marching up and down outside the cinema, shouting that the film was a slur and that there *were* no gay Asians. But you can understand where they were coming from since there had been virtually no representation of Asians in the media. The answer is more diverse representation which the film helped to establish, I hope. In the end, you can't write to anybody else's ideas. If other people think Asians should be represented in a certain way, then they can write their own stories.

*You have also been a target for those who argue you create stereo-
types of fundamentalist Muslims in* My Son The Fanatic. *How
would you answer their charges? Do you feel the need to?*

Well, there are as many kinds of Muslim as there are Christians,
obviously. I just write about the small corner of the world that
interests me. I never claim to create a full picture. I just do what I
do. The self censorship goes on all the time, to do with issues of
style, taste, judgement, character. But I would never try to imagine
what the world might want or not want. To try to fit in with it would
prevent you from writing anything. For example, does the world
want a film about a gay Nazi running a launderette? The work
creates the market rather than the other way around, as with, for
example, postcolonial writing where the works create the interest
and the label comes later. When you imagine a mixed-race Asian
living in the South London suburbs, you can't ask if anyone *wants*
to read about him because no one *has* previously written about him,
so you can't know.

*Your humour is earthy, salty, farcical at times. Can you say some-
thing about humour, in* Buddha *especially?*

I guess you develop your humour from your family, out of the sense
of humour your parents have. But I also grew up on British sitcoms.
When you're sitting at home in Bromley you tend to mostly watch
Dad's Army and *On the Buses* and *Please, Sir!* and all that stuff.
That was the humour of my time. In Bromley you didn't go and
watch films directed by Godard, you watched *On the Buses!* My
humour is very British in that sense. Any writer's humour comes
from the sort of person you are — just as your whole style, the
language you use, the characters you create — comes from your own
character and how you see the world. The humour in my work has
certainly changed over the years. *The Buddha of Suburbia* is a
comic novel in a way that *Intimacy* quite clearly is not. Humour

depends on your mood, on what the subject is, and on what you're thinking about at the time. I think the humour in *Buddha* comes from the point of view of a young man. When you're a kid adults are hilarious, your teachers all seem to have one leg and one eye and they're just funny. And you sort of deconstruct the world as a kid: you deconstruct the power and authority of the world by mocking it. People's parents are very funny to their kids. My children just look at me and they laugh. They think that the things I do are hilarious and I don't realise that I'm doing anything that might be conceived as funny. You can see the same things happening through the generations: you are just as idiotic to them as your parents were to you and so on. When you become the teacher yourself—when you become middle-aged and have only got one eye and one leg yourself—it is not so funny and the world becomes more complicated and more painful.

Memory and history seem to play an important role for you.

I think the history you remember is first and foremost your parents' lives: my father's life in India, my mother's during the Second World War. They were two quite different people coming together after the War in a bombed out London, then having my sister and I and worrying about how we would fit in. Then there was the racism of the 1960s and Enoch Powell. Where your own life and that of your family intersects with general history is significant in terms of personal, psychological and social history. I would say my father was the key influence.

In Intimacy *you write: "The dream or nightmare of the happy family haunts us all. It is one of the few utopian ideas we have these days." Are you writing in part against the fetishisation of the nuclear family?*

I was thinking the other day about the idea of the family that we grew up with in the 1950s and 1960s. The idea of the family that my generation had inherited was really breaking up by the 1980s when people like Margaret Thatcher and Ronald Reagan began to proselytize it. I remember being very puzzled by why Ronald Reagan and Margaret Thatcher in particular went on and on about the family. The whole idea of family in that period was clearly breaking down and that is partly chronicled in *The Buddha of Suburbia* and later more seriously and in other ways in the other books. It was probably a fantasy in the first place. The whole idea rested on the woman being at home and the man going out to work while the kids were at school. There are very few people who live in that precise way in nuclear families.

In the early work there are alternative "families" — communes like Jamila's house in Buddha, *Danny/Victoria's trailer site in* Sammy and Rosie *and the posse in* London Kills Me. *Do you see the nuclear family mediating into other forms — strangers or social outcasts coming together? Are you testing the boundaries of the "family"?*

Growing up in the 1950s and 1960s and being involved on the Left, and with hippies, I was very aware that my mates were thinking about new ways of living, particularly in that period after university and before usually you have kids yourself. I knew a lot of people living in housing associations, other people in communes and others involved in all kinds of other sexual relationships, for instance, particularly the Gay Movement in the 1970s. I was very interested and involved in thinking about whether there were other ways in which to live without living in the traditional nuclear family. But I think people are still hypnotized by that idea. I don't think it's much of a reality and it's a dangerous idea in lots of ways because it makes people feel like failures. That is how "family" has often been used, particularly by Margaret Thatcher: to make people in single families think that they were not as good as those in traditional families. I was extremely interested in the ways that the family was used politically in the 1980s.

One cultural critic has argued that if we could stop the fetishizing of the family unit, homesick fathers might have a better hearing.[3] *It seems to me that the non-custodial parent, still almost always the father, is a figure you have begun to rescue from obscurity in your recent work.*

I think that before feminism it was a bad deal: men got the work and the women got the kids and there wasn't much sharing either way. So, the women missed out on the work and the men missed out on the kids. In a way under Thatcherism a lot of that changed, partly because of mass unemployment because men were at home and women did other kinds of work to make do. Inadvertently, people were able to experiment with different modes of living. I guess I'm interested in men because I'm a bloke myself but also because I was very interested in the revolutions of my time: for gays, women, blacks and Asians—with people becoming aware of their positions. And white blokes got rather left out of that. But of course when everybody else's position changed so the white bloke's position changed as well. So I try to write from his point of view as well.

So, is a feature of your writing agenda a study of masculinity in crisis? I'm thinking of Stephen in Sleep With Me *and Roger in* "Umbrellas," *for example.*

I think as a writer you look for the moment of crisis because it is so dramatic. When you think about how you're going to construct a text, you think of the moment when something is breaking down and you'll go in at that point. Say, in the film *My Son the Fanatic* where the main character is a taxi-driver: you look for the moment when his life is falling apart because for a writer that is dramatic. You look for the moment when he has to make lots of difficult decisions about who he wants to be. It's partly to do with craft, about where you start a story and about what you look for and where the story begins: where do you start? Where do you go in? It is about looking for the moment when somebody's life is falling apart and they have to think about who they are, what they believe and who they want to be and what sort of relationships they have. You can enter a marriage that is in crisis and think what do these people really want. Who do they want to be now? As a writer I try to go in at that point of crisis and then I can go back or forward and see what's happening.

Are specific objects sometimes a symbolic or metaphorical focus (Clint's search for shoes in London Kills Me, *the umbrella, "The Penis," the turd in "Tale of the Turd") Are they an imaginative and associative starting point?*

It's not something that I'm particularly aware of. . . . Maupassant is a writer I've always really loved. I've never really thought about things or objects quite in that way. I love absurdity and in *The Black Album* there's the aubergine so there are symbols or objects in my work. But, to be honest, I've not really thought of it in that way.

How do you feel about critical labels being attached to you, then? I'm thinking specifically of your work being labelled "postcolonial." Is it a term you can embrace?

It's something you have to live with. It is going to happen. You write stuff and send it out and people are going to do things with it. That's fine and up to them but if you try to engage with them then that's when it gets difficult. For example, I can't think about myself as a postcolonial writer. When I go upstairs to my study, I think "what do I want to write about today?" I can't think about myself or my work theoretically. I have to go to a concrete object: two people fighting over an umbrella, as you say. Then the writing comes alive. There are two aspects to writing: one is the creative aspect and the other is that it is a business in the sense that I have to support my family and that's the side of it where I send stuff out into the world and people make of it what they will. I think the postcolonial label has always bothered me slightly because, to me, it is a narrow term. And so much of my work is not about that and so you feel that you're being squashed into a category that you don't quite fit and you fear that there are lots of other aspects of your work which people might then be ignoring. But I'm not going to get hung up about that or bother about it too much. Perhaps people will get bored with postcolonialism and carry on reading my stuff. I don't think of V. S. Naipaul as a colonial or postcolonial writer, I think of him in the same way as I think of Graham Greene. They're both great writers.

Are there descriptors that you feel more closely define you as a writer? Would you be happier being described as a chronicler of London?

I like London and I like what goes on here. I'm interested in the idea of opening the door and not knowing whom you are going to meet or what's going to happen. Also, being a suburban boy, I've never lost the romance of London: the idea of coming to London and it always being exciting and it always being dull in the suburbs which to me as a teenager it was. Writers have to be interested in the inside of people — their minds — and in the outside — the world — and the conjunction of those two things. The city has always turned me on. There's always something else I want to describe. For example, writing about the 1980s, the film world, Soho, the advertising business that I haven't written about yet. I think what is great about the novel is that you can go anywhere with it and do anything. It seems to me to be a wonderful form, almost better than any other form for conveying human experience. You can go into people's minds, the intricacies of their minds, describe shops, streets, anything. If I read a book about Paris in the nineteenth century I like those bits, the descriptive sections. The novel is the most capacious, the most sensual form.

So how do you feel when a novel is transferred to the screen? In the adaptation of Buddha, *the first person narration is lost. Do other aspects concern you?*

The language is lost and for writers it's the most important thing. All writers go to a lot of trouble to put their words in a certain order and to catch the right words where possible, and of course, you lose that. But you gain lots of other things too. You get to see actors' faces, you get to see good acting, good directing, when you see the text as a movie. I've always worked in film so it's not as if I feel that film is necessarily a degradation of the work. I thought Roger Michell did a really good job with the TV version of *Buddha* and it worked very well. Now when I think of *Buddha*, I see the actors and the text is mediated through them. The actors have become superimposed on the text.

You have compiled an ensemble, a cast of characters, and had some important collaborative relationships too, haven't you?

I have been lucky to work with some tip-top people in the theatre and in film: Howard Davis, Max Stafford-Clarke, Stephen Frears, Patrice Chereau, Udayan Prasad. You have to rework, compromise, change when working with directors and I need the argument and the criticism to test my work. I enjoy good and important fights over material and I've enjoyed working with a set of actors who are associated with my work, like Roshan Seth, Naveen Andrews, Rita

Wolf, Meera Syal, Steve Mackintosh. I've got a new film coming up called *The Mother* that Steve Macintosh might be in. It's a dull life being a writer so working in film and the theatre with actors is cheering and inspiring.

You have also compiled a cast of characters who reappear?

In *Gabriel's Gift* especially. I think you become really fond of them, you get to like them. They're all parts of your own self in some way but you also wonder how they develop and age. I guess what I'm interested in is time and how people change over time. I'd like to know what Karim is doing now or what Charlie Hero is really like now. It is inspiring for me to imagine what might have happened to them so I write about a character I created years ago. I like the fact that the audience is interested too so you have a relationship with those readers who recognise what you are doing. I usually write a group of pieces around a subject, like *The Black Album* and "My Son the Fanatic" which go together. There's a short story, "Night Light" that goes with "Sleep With Me" and *Intimacy*, then there's *Buddha* and *My Beautiful Laundrette*. I tend to write around the same subject for a bit until I feel that I've said what I want to say. You circle around, rather like a painter who might do a sketch, a sculpture and a painting of the same subject, a face or a body, and experiment with the subject for a while before moving on to something else.

You have also said that you measured out your life in pop music and that consequently music forms part of your cultural vocabulary. Can you say more about this?

I did at the beginning. I don't think I do so much now. It was so liberating for us at that time. Music was linked to so many other things, not just fashion but politics — in Eastern Europe and in the United States — the straight world, the weird world. It meant so much. Then, when I was writing *The Black Album*, I was listening to a lot of Prince and Madonna. It was a time in the 1980s when ambiguous sexuality was moving into the mainstream and subcultures were becoming mainstream. It was very odd how the Thatcherite-Reaganite energy was absorbing the weirdo stuff, turning people on to it but at the same time rendering it innocuous. Music can take you anywhere. I had been interested in The Beatles but I hadn't heard Little Richard. So then I listened to him and to John Lee Hooker, and to other black music of the 1950s. You begin with one thing and take up others. You might say that all culture works by appropriation. There's me, an Asian kid sitting in Bromley in my bedroom listening to The Rolling Stones who appropriated black music and at the same time I am reading James Baldwin. I'm in a sense reappropriating it when it comes to figure in *Buddha*, having been influenced by all this other stuff as well. Clearly, you have to say there are all kinds of distinctions to be made about appropriation.

There are certain signature scenes, moments or phrases that occur across stories too. Is this conscious?

Some of it is unconscious and some of it is deliberate. I think the stuff in *Intimacy* and "Sleep with Me" is deliberate. I was playing with ideas. You have to write them out, release them.

Thinking about Intimacy, *we wondered whether it is really more about desire than intimacy? In* "Blue, Blue Pictures of You" *you actually have a character who considers writing "a book of desire."*

It is about the *dream* of intimacy rather like we were talking about the dream of the family—or a fantasy of a certain kind of family. It is the idea or ideal that you might have that haunts you that you pursue but never quite catch up with. So, therefore, the story is about failed intimacy or the desire for intimacy. It is certainly about desire but what it is a desire *for* I'm not entirely sure: certainly for recognition rather than union, being recognised, being seen, being understood. The film is an adult film. I always thought it should have a 35 certificate! It is quite a dark film, not a film for eighteen-year-olds eating popcorn. Films at the moment seem to be so formulaic. When you see a film like this, it feels dark, strange, and very unusual.

Interviewed in the Guardian, *Alexander Linklater the partner of Kerry Fox the actress in* Intimacy, *described the film as an example of "sublime ugliness." What would you say to that?*

I have just written an essay about the film, "The Two Of Us." It is really about Patrice Chereau and I was thinking about people like Bacon and Freud, about flesh — real flesh as opposed to advertising flesh — the idealisation and use of sex in the media that seems to be corrupt, as opposed to what bodies and sexuality are really like in real people which I try to write about more seriously. This film is more like that — more like a Lucien Freud painting and that's the ugliness. There are real human bodies and real people, real struggles over desire that you don't usually see in the cinema. It is a composite of "Night Light," "Strangers When We Meet" and *Love in a Blue Time.* I told Chereau to take what he wanted from the works and then we sat around and worked out a story. I did the story in that sense.

Desire has been seen as the location of resistance to convention through transgressive sexualities and relationships, drug-fuelled passion, pornography. Is that how you conceive of desire — or is it simply a utopian project?

I think that all western literature is probably about desire so it is a broad subject in that sense. *Anna Karenina* is all about desire and so is *Madame Bovary.* It is question of people wanting things very badly which often comes down to people wanting other people very badly. The literature then being an exploration of the way that your desire for other people is always constrained by the society, in that you are not allowed to desire certain people, certain things.

You could say that **Anna Karenina** *and* **Tess of the D'Urbervilles** *are constrained by romance plots, though, while you are not limited in that precise way.*

That's an interesting thing to say. The form of the novel has changed and I'm also working across a number of genres. What is common is the idea that desire is transgressive, as you say: Madame Bovary does not love her husband but she does love people who are not her husband. In *My Son The Fanatic* the main character is no longer in love with his wife but he loves a prostitute which is transgressive in itself. But what should we make of it? It becomes not only an emotional, sexual problem but a social problem too and that is when a novelist gets interested and worried and starts to think about how desire works in society, not only in the minds and bodies of the people involved. That's a question that we are all interested in: what do we do with desire? What shapes does it follow and how does it run? How transgressive does it have to be to continue to be exciting? For Freud all desire is transgressive and incestuous.

In your early work desire is set against impending social crisis as in **Sammy and Rosie** *and* **My Beautiful Laundrette***. But with the later work there is a stronger emphasis on the interior worlds of the characters, isn't there?*

I suppose different kinds of desire are transgressive and dangerous in different ways. Let's say being gay in London today is not like being gay in Afghanistan so it depends where you locate the characters. During the 1980s, Thatcher, it seemed to a lot of us, was trying to introduce, in shorthand, "old-fashioned morals."

Therefore, transgressive desire seemed very important to write about then. So you combine two gay blokes running a launderette, which is the entrepreneurship she wanted, and you make it transgressive. The social stuff *has* fallen away to a certain extent. Also my work has got pared down. I think that often does happen to artists: you become very interested in economy, doing things as economically as you can, and the wrong word, or too many words, offends you. I think you look for new styles. I am much more interested in a piece of writing that is broken up, fragmented, unfinished. Sometimes I look at my notes and think why would I even bother to organise these notes into a fluid page. I like the spaces between the notes. I leave three spaces between this chunk of prose and the next. I like it looking like that on the page. You show it to people and they tell you that you can't publish it as it is not "written" yet. But it is the fact that it is *not* written that interests me. Then, to follow through, you may be moving away from the public. I guess my writing has always been quite conventional. I start at the beginning and move all the way through — just like the novels I read as I grew up — or the way I thought they worked. But now I am much more interested in the experimental, not for its own sake but because I like the look of the words on the page in that way — the gaps, the unfinished bits. The writing is like some of the later work of Miles Davis: it sounds cacophonous to other people. It may sound like banging on pots but it is interesting to Davis. It is quite difficult, particularly when you are an established writer, to decide how far you can go in terms of your relationship with the audience. I liked *Intimacy* being a rough book in that sense; the cruelty, the fragmentation, the lack of smoothing out or over. People have said the book is so cruel and horrible, the people in it are so nasty and I say "well, that's what it's like." I wanted the book to be an experience. If I wrote a book now about a relationship that split up ten years ago, it would probably be overworked and too thought-out. I wanted to capture the roughness. The style you use has to reflect what is going on in the mind at the time of writing.

You have begun to exploit new technology as with your website.

I guess so. Websites are good for certain things. You can publish stories and bits and pieces on them. Websites are great in that you can write something and bang it up straightaway but people don't really know it is there unless you go to a lot of trouble to advertise. Books are still best. But you get a lag with books. I've got two books that my publisher hasn't yet got around to publishing that will turn up after a while. You have to plan an advertising campaign and go to bookshops. "Goodbye Mother," a story that was published in *Granta*, is now on my site. But I don't think I would put a novel on there.

Would you mind talking about unpublished work?

I have completed a novel called *The Body* and I would like to write another book about race, starting from the 1970s and coming up to the present day. I thought it might be a saga but my books are getting shorter and more condensed. My work, as I say, is becoming really concentrated and I don't write the bits I don't choose to. How much should you explain? Will the audience move through the ideas with you? These kinds of questions don't go away as you continue into your writing career.

Do you feel you are picking up new readers with short stories?

Maybe. It is hard for me to get a sense of the readership. Sometimes I will go to a reading but I don't get much idea of the specific audience. Reviews don't tell you much about your readership either. It is not like sitting in a cinema where you can see and feel people responding to the film you have made. But, I did a reading in Leeds recently and there were a few men who were talking about being separated from their wives and children and of the relationships they try — and sometimes fail — to build with them both. It did give me a sense that people might look for that stuff in my work.

At one juncture in the screenplay for **Sammy and Rosie Get Laid** *you say that you are "no good at plots, at working out precisely what the story is." How significant is plot in your writing?*

I am interested in movement and change, in development in a person or character. Plot is a much more mechanical unfolding according to some preconceived plan which I can never quite do. I'm writing and then I think, wouldn't it be great if so-and-so happened now and I go off in another direction, often this seems disjointed or weird. With *Sammy and Rosie* the film moves all over the place and I rather like that. In a sense there are two sides to me: wanting the work to be crafted and liking to do weird things in the work. In *Gabriel's Gift* a painting comes to life and Gabriel speaks with his dead brother, for example. Really in that novel the weird aspects have to do with somebody going mad because their parents have split up and Gabriel wants to be an artist but is unable to move outside of his own head. Later in the book, Gabriel stops feeling crazy because he begins to relate to other people and to the world outside. It is important to be part of wider relations. It is rather like being a writer: if you sit up in your office imagining for long enough, your relationship with the rest of the world could become tenuous. So you keep sane by having relationships.

So Gabriel is rescued by the relationship he has with his father which socialises him?

Yes, and he is rescued by his general ability to make friends with other people. I think the writing always has to exist in relationship to others or it becomes obsessive, circular. It is not just self-expression. Literary form is important too as recognised by others.

You conceived of Gabriel's Gift *as a children's book, didn't you?*

Yes, in that David Bowie wanted a book that he could then illustrate, but as I was writing it became more of an adult book. I have written one children's story, "Ladybirds For Tea." I think when you have children, you want to write for them and it wouldn't occur to you otherwise.

Do you feel Gabriel's Gift *re-established you after the controversy of* Intimacy?

Intimacy really bothers people where *Gabriel's Gift* does not. I think some reviewers were caught up in the furore around *Intimacy* and so haven't yet looked fairly and squarely at the book. Nor have they yet taken into consideration the fact that I was aware I was playing a literary game. I consciously wrote *Intimacy* in the form of a confession and was also aware that it might be read as "Hanif Kureishi telling the truth about a relationship break-up." That too is a literary construct: it is artificial. All of one's work is autobiographical to the extent that it reflects one's interests. But the book hasn't yet been read as a move in a literary game which is quite disappointing. It operates as a construct—written in the first person, constructed as a confession—and this is the basis on which it should begin to be evaluated. I wanted a book people could play with in that way. It is a text, not me. I am not the text.

Does the cult of celebrity annoy you then? If you weren't famous, critics wouldn't have read the novel as autobiography and you do have that ironic scene in the story "That Was Then" *when Natasha challenges Nick for using her life in his book.*

I suppose it works both ways. Being a celebrity allows you to write books that people will read, which is what we all want. But, on the other hand, it devalues what you do, as all celebrity does. It makes it one-dimensional.

The last section of Gabriel's Gift *is a kind of coda — a happy ending. In reclaiming what is comfortable at the heart of many families, it is perhaps the happiest ending you have written, isn't it?*

There aren't any happy endings in life but there are happy moments. Other pieces are cheerful too, like "Four Blue Chairs." What you want as a writer is to write in different tones for your own pleasure. It isn't as if any one thing you write is your final testament. *Intimacy* isn't how I am feeling today, or even how I felt the day after it was finished. It isn't my last word on marriage, relationships, children. You write in light and dark.

2

The Novel

The *Buddha of Suburbia* tells politically-nuanced and hugely comical stories about contemporary Britain. Published in 1990, it was a novel ahead of its time. Its British protagonist of biracial heritage only found a category to tick on the national census form in 2001, and the appellation "mixed race" still conveys little of the complex history of ethnic encounters in the UK with which Kureishi engages. Hanif Kureishi's first novel uncovers many of the ironies that underlie our recognition of Britain as a multicultural society and of Britons as racially diverse and culturally heterogeneous citizens. Kureishi sets his novel in London where around 300 different languages are currently spoken. In 2001, the (then) British Foreign Secretary Robin Cook declared chicken tikka masala a "true British national dish" in an effort to promote Britain's cultural harmony in the year in which the British National Party secured their best ever result in a General Election.[4] Multicultural Britain remains at the forefront of public and media attention into the new millennium, and this novel set in the 1970s touches on many issues that remain as controversial as they are comic. It provides food for cultural and political thought all at the same time.

In Karim, Kureishi creates a seventeen-year-old boy and follows him over four years in the 1970s, during which he falls in and out of love and tries on a host of different identities (from self-imposed to imposed). He witnesses the breakdown of his parents' marriage, the unconventional "marriage" of his friend Jamila, and the transformation of his father into a "Buddha" of the South London suburbs. The latter is not the only transformation that takes place: the love of Karim's young life, Charlie, echoes the mood of the late 1970s when he embarks on a career as a punk in London and New York. Much of the action takes place on the urban fringes of popular culture, and much of the humor rests on the ways in which these lower middle-class boys negotiate new lives outside of the safe suburban setting that is their typically English home. The whole is a rollercoaster of a novel; funny, ironic, and archly knowing.

The Buddha of Suburbia is a lively, busy novel — two novels even, since the two sections "In the Suburbs" and "In the City" are arguably synonymous with a short first novel and its sequel. Its primary settings, the South London suburbs, most specifically Bromley and Central London, give way to New York for a short but significant section. However, in the main, the novel focuses on life in Britain, reworking Disraeli's "two nations" of the Victorian rich and poor as center and margin, metropolitan and suburban.[5] Kureishi is clearly interested in multiple conceptions of England. The "England" he describes is contradictory and duplicitous at times. One is reminded of a writer he admires, J. B. Priestley, and his famous statement "I had seen a lot of Englands." In his essay "Bradford," Kureishi notes the importance of Bradford-born Priestley's "three Englands": the "traditional" guide book England of cathedrals and countryside, industrial England, and suburban (Americanized) England, and Kureishi adds a fourth, the inner city. Kureishi has stated elsewhere that the inner city represents the evanescent fads and phases of contemporary British life; in contrast to living quietly with the family in the suburbs, in the inner city London that Kureishi takes as his subject, "People came and went. There was much false intimacy and forced friendship. People didn't take responsibility for each other." Reading *The Buddha of Suburbia*, one is made aware of the dialectical relationship between freedom and commitment, politics and sexuality, but each politicized point is deftly crafted as farce. The idea of Britain Kureishi wills into being lampoons many of the old established tropes of English life and leads the reader to reflect on new ways of seeing a nation they may feel they know well.

BUDDHA: A VERY ENGLISH NOVEL

It is worth noting that when foreign students study in England, institutions and organizers, like the ISA-Butler program, recommend *The Buddha of Suburbia* as a novel they should read to aid orientation, "to get a feel for the country." Kureishi has dryly described his first novel as "Kingsley Amis meets the Velvet Underground." Amis's novel *Lucky Jim* (1953) has as its protagonist "Lucky" Jim Dixon, an enduring figure within the English literary tradition who is a curious admixture of self-centerd pretense and a clumsy desire to belong. English fiction is renowned for its unapologetically eccentric ex-centrics, its outsiders as heroes. D. J. Taylor believes characters populating the novels of Martin Amis and James Kelman fulfill that role but finds them lacking in the qualities readers found in Kingsley Amis's Jim. He might be as well to examine Kureishi's protagonist, Karim Amir, for a witty exploration of the complexities of living in Britain in the 1970s.

Kureishi is more of the satirist. On *The Late Show* in 1990, he described himself as "in some ways quite a traditional English comic writer who happens to be dealing with subjects that are considered by some to be dangerous, like drugs and certain sexual practices." Setting himself up in this way steals a march on those who may unquestioningly assume an English writer will be ethnically undifferentiated as "white." On the novel's publication, his interviewers on television shows like *The Late Show* and *Rear Window* certainly focused on *The Buddha of Suburbia*'s location within a British fictional tradition, with one interviewer referring to Kureishi as "an Asian John Mortimer" after the creator of the popular comic character Rumpole of the Bailey. Novelist Angela Carter asserted "Karim's story will prove to be most English in its heritage, that of the glorious, scabrous, picaresque, savage, sentimental tradition of low comedy that stretches from Chaucer to the dirty postcards on Brighton Pier." Another critic, Alamgir Hashmi, spends most of his article exemplifying Kureishi's indebtedness to an English literary tradition, comparing *Buddha* to works by H. G. Wells and Angus Wilson and various other novels of "social focus eased by a comic outlook."

However, even when located within a comic tradition, Kureishi's work remains controversial, not solely as a result of its sexual content but as a result of its clearly anti-Thatcherite stance. Prior to the publication of this novel, Kureishi's ideological position was made clear in plays and in the films *My Beautiful Laundrette* and *Sammy and Rosie Get Laid*. Stephen Frears, whose directing career might be reasonably described as anti-establishment, has described the films he directed in the 1980s, including those with Kureishi, as "films shrieking at Mrs. Thatcher." The right-wing Oxford historian Norman Stone infamously criticized a number of such films for what he called an "overall feeling of disgust and decay," a response to British society that he believed "worthless and insulting." The venomous tirade in which he celebrates "very good films of a traditional kind," like *Passage to India, Room With A View,* and *Hope and Glory* and decimates *My Beautiful Laundrette* and *Sammy and Rosie*, falls into a national myth of British life as resolutely traditional and ethnically undifferentiated. Stone's British community romanticizes the history of Empire that denies the hybridity of British identity underpinning the dynamics of the films he attacks. Kureishi, in his response to Stone ("England, bloody England"), points out that E. M. Forster, writer of two of the three novels on which Stone's favorite films are based, was himself a controversial and dissenting individual. Salman Rushdie's comment that the success of "Raj revisionism" is "the artistic counterpart to the rise of conservative ideologies in modern Britain" helps to clarify Stone's reactionary attack, and to contextualize just why Kureishi's representations of English life may hit a nerve.

Stone is an example of the rear guard action that right-wing apologists mounted in the 1980s to help to preserve a myth of harmonious "Englishness" in the face of that decade's political and social realities. It is difficult to consider *The Buddha of Suburbia*, published at the end of that decade, without also countering Stone's criticisms since Kureishi's work emerges from what Iain Chambers has called "the inventive edges of the consensus, from the previously ignored and suppressed." In Chambers's definition the inventiveness comprises of "a widening democratization" of styles and images reflecting "new possibilities, new perspectives, new projects." Kureishi provides new perspectives on myths of Englishness and nationhood and attendant problems of nationalism. Film critic Sheila Johnson, examining representations of "Britishness" via *Chariots of Fire* and *Ploughman's Lunch* (one would assume that Norman Stone would enjoy the former but revile the latter), identifies the 1980s as "an historical moment when notions of national unity were once again being dusted down and re-mobilised in the interests of political expediency." Most significantly for our context, Johnson expresses the hope that subsequent cultural productions "will continue to move away from hoary national mythologies and conventional narrative formats."

When Kureishi shifts his attention to fiction with *Buddha*, he undermines the same national myths he satirizes so successfully in his screenplays: those that derive from lower middle-class white social mores and those that derive from the etiquette of immigrant groups. Karim's Auntie Jean and Uncle Ted (Gin and Tonic as Haroon calls them) have prided themselves on their "dos," garden parties where the air is "thick with aftershave and perfume," and while Karim's mother hopes to go unnoticed, his father Haroon "liked to stand out like a juggler at a funeral" (42). When Kureishi distinguishes between social groups he avoids limiting them by assumptions about cultural designation. When Jamila and Changez marry, the dowry he demands reflects the character's own idiosyncracies rather than the ways in which he might represent his ethnic and cultural group: "the ageing boy had demanded a warm winter overcoat from Moss Bros., a colour television and, mysteriously, an edition of the complete works of Conan Doyle." This prompts Haroon to ask "What normal Indian man would want such a thing? The boy must be investigated further — immediately!" (57)

Kureishi edges into satire most effectively when he confronts the sheer banality of quotidian life for most Britons most of the time. Most of those who live in Karim's neighborhood are in bed by 10:30 pm and most kids his age lead what he calls "a steady life in my bedroom with my radio" (94). The predominant emotion is boredom. Charlie Hero finds it easy to accuse Karim of "looking English" when he is at his most awkward and reserved: "So shocked, so self-righteous and moral, so loveless and incapable of dancing. They are narrow, the English. It's a Kingdom of Prejudice over there. Don't be like it!" (254). Even though Charlie is embarking on a session of sado-masochistic sex, he still feels able to take the "high ground" by contrasting himself to the rest of "the English."

When Kureishi published *Buddha* he helped to fill what he has called "a hole in the centre of English writing," a gap about the lives and experiences of Black peoples in Britain or, in Kobena Mercer's terms, he performs "the role of making present what had been rendered absent." Kureishi follows Orwell for whom class was the hole waiting to be filled and, like Orwell, he takes stands on certain issues. He has drawn readers' attention on many occasions to his repeated readings of George Orwell's 1944 essay "England Your England." Following Orwell, among others, Kureishi admitted the difficulties of identifying himself with England's colonialist history and myths of nationhood in the early essay "The Rainbow Sign" (1986). It is precisely this sense of dislocation that has led to his becoming consistently tenacious in exploring precisely what it is to be British, and how that complex citizenship might be represented. Kureishi remembers "I wasn't a misfit; I could join the elements of myself together. It was the others, they wanted misfits; they wanted you to embody within yourself their ambivalence." Kureishi and, by extension, Karim, has few problems in identifying with even the most traditional features of British life. One thinks of Karim's disquisition on the joys of drinking tea and cycling (62) and of the things he values about Uncle Ted: "We ate corned-beef sandwiches and drank tea from our thermos flask. He gave me sporting tips and took me to the Catford dog track and Epsom Downs. He talked to me about pigeon racing. . . . fishing and air rifles, aeroplanes, and how to eat winkles" (33). Kureishi remembers his grandfather's influence on his childhood as "pigeon-keeping, greyhound racing, roast beef eating and pianos in pubs." He is quite clear that:

It is the British, the white British, who have to learn that being British isn't what it was. Now it is a more complex thing, involving new elements. So there must be a fresh way of seeing Britain and the choices it faces: and a new way of being British after all this time. Much thought, discussion and self-examination must go into seeing the necessity for this, what this "new way of being British" involves and how difficult it might be to attain.

The failure to grasp this opportunity for a revitalized and broader self-definition in the face of a real failure to be human, will be more insularity, schism, bitterness and catastrophe.

Kureishi's statement here could be said to serve as an alternative articulation of what Kobena Mercer believes is the predicament of contemporary black British cultural producers: "If, after many years of struggle, you arrive at the threshold of enunciation and are 'given' the-right-to speak and a limited space in which to tell your story, is it not the case that there will be an overwhelming pressure to try and tell the whole story at once?" Kureishi does not bend to the pressure to tell everything about Britain at once, although like Orwell he seems to exclaim "And the diversity of it, the chaos!" Kureishi confronts the difficulty of being able to convey his fresh way of seeing Britain effectively when as Orwell noted, "In left-wing circles it is always felt that there is something slightly disgraceful in being an Englishman and that it is a duty to snigger at every English institution, from horse-racing to suet puddings." Kureishi has Cherry, a Pakistani woman living in London, snigger that "this silly little island off Europe" could never be home, while in the *Buddha* Changez refers to an "unfriendly cold England" (101). But in *Buddha,* it is the comedy inherent in Karim's position as "an (almost) Englishman" that drives both the plot and much of the political satire. "The Rainbow Sign," where he begins to outline his ideas and beliefs, derives its title from James Baldwin's important essay collection *The Fire Next Time* (1963), "God gave Noah the rainbow sign/ No more water, the fire next time!" When one reads Kureishi through the African-American writer and activist, it becomes clear that, even at its comic heart, the political thrust of *Buddha* involves a warning that if British society continues to marginalize racism rather than tackle the problem, there will be dire social consequences.

Kureishi, then, perceives his writing as located firmly within a British context where establishing a *conceptually* British identity that incorporates ethnic and cultural differences is an ultimate aim. Roy Jenkins, as Home Secretary in the Labour government, expressed a similar view as long ago as 1966:

I do not think we need in this country a melting pot, which will turn everybody out in a common mould, as one of a series of carbon copies of someone's misplaced vision of the stereotyped Englishman. . . . I define integration, therefore, not as a flattening process of assimilation but as equal opportunity, coupled with cultural diversity, in an atmosphere of mutual tolerance.

Kureishi outlines his belief that contemporary British fiction is a space in which such issues may be explored:

If contemporary writing which emerges from oppressed groups ignores the central concerns and major conflicts of the larger society, it will automatically designate itself as minor, as a sub-genre. And it must not allow itself to be rendered invisible and marginalised in this way.

His England is clear-eyed and unpatriotic: even though, and again like Orwell, he allows that suet puddings and red pillar boxes have entered his soul, his context is post imperial and post-industrial, and rarely nostalgic.

LONDON AND SUBURBIA

London almost always figures largely in Kureishi's writing, as he points out in the interview that opens this book. He has said "I'm no Britisher, but a Londoner" on more than one occasion. London is his special subject; the city functioning, on the one hand, as a metonym for a complex and heterogeneous British Isles and, on the other, as a precise location for his characters. Kureishi, like Angela Carter in fiction like *Wise Children* (1992), a novel Salman Rushdie described as "a raspberry blown by South London across the Thames," begins his first novel in the South London suburbs and, again following Carter, Kureishi can be described as a "thumber of noses, a defiler of sacred cows." There is little in Kureishi's London that is calm or time-honored. *Sammy and Rosie Get Laid* includes a paean to the city in which Sammy's voiceover comments on a collage of bohemian scenes:

On Saturdays we like to walk along the towpath at Hammersmith and kiss and argue.

(Next we see Sammy and Rosie in 'Any Amount of Books'.)

(Voice over) Then we go to the bookshop and buy novels written by women.

(Next, Sammy and Rosie outside the Albert Hall.)

(Voiceover) Or we trot past the Albert Hall and up through Hyde Park. On Saturday nights things really hot up. . . .

We go to an Alternative Cabaret in Earl's Court in the hope of seeing our government abused. . . .

We love our city and we belong to it. Neither of us are English, we're Londoners you see.

Kureishi's London is an eclectic educated mix for accountant Sammy and social worker Rosie. Whereas for Karim the bohemian gives way to a fascination with the seedy:

So this was London at last, and nothing gave me more pleasure than strolling around my new possession all day. London seemed like a house with five thousand rooms, all different; the kick was to work out how they were connected. . . . There were small hotels smelling of spunk and disinfectant, Australian travel agents, all-night shops run by dwarfish Bengalis, leather bars with fat moustached queens exchanging secret signals outside, and roaming strangers with no money and searching eyes. In Kensington nobody looked at you. In Earls Court everybody did, wondering what they could wrench from you. (126–127)

As Kureishi continues to publish, his literary London becomes more expansive. The short story "The Umbrella" is anthologized in a special issue of *Granta* called "London, the Lives of the City" and in the film *Intimacy* the capital feels lonely, even brutal, with quietly desperate characters seeking sexual intimacy amid its bleakness.

In *Sammy and Rosie*, Sammy explains to his father that London is *the* place to live since it is cosmopolitan and cheap. Neither Kureishi nor his characters are rootless cosmopolitans though; they are often Londoners born and bred and, apart from *My Son the Fanatic* set in Bradford and the play *Sleep With Me* located in the Gloucestershire countryside, even Kureishi's "dual-location" writings like "With Your Tongue Down My Throat" are set in Pakistan — *and* London. Kureishi's London is not the same kind of "city within a city" as Sam Selvon's lonely Trinidadian Londoners inhabit in Bayswater and Brixton, or Timothy Mo's Chinatown in *Sour Sweet* (1982). Rather than an immigrant enclave, Karim's London is more reliant on popular cultural images of the 1960s that persist into the 1970s: music, TV, theater. In *Buddha* the city is overblown and unrestrained, sexy and cheap, grotesque and theatrical, "an inferno of pleasure and madness," as Kureishi recently described London in an interview. For Karim it epitomizes the best of all possible worlds in which to take his faltering but exciting steps from adolescence to adulthood. When one remembers that Angela Carter referred to Karim as a version of Voltaire's Candide, the Panglossian reference to "the best of all possible worlds" takes on a specifically literary resonance. Kureishi seems tagged with such references: one critic even referring to him as a Dickensian "artful dodger."

In many ways the New York where Karim and Charlie spend the last few chapters of the novel is as much a postmodern extension of their popular cultural fantasies as it is a firm geo-cultural location. Much of New York's artistic scene passes in an aimless drunken haze. Charlie's rock persona is "temporary, borrowed" and his music has "lost its drama and attack when transported from England with its unemployment, strikes and class antagonism" (246–7). As soon as he begins living in New York, Charlie acquires a Cockney accent, when Karim's memory of him is as a boy at school who "cried after being mocked for talking so posh." Karim is in no doubt: "Charlie is 'selling Englishness' "(247). Charlie's striking of this pose reflects something of the fluidity and popular cultural currency of working class markers and echoes Johnny in *My Beautiful Laundrette*, whose position within the British community is also unstable and shifting; he moves from marching with the National Front through Lewisham to working for Omar and being one of Nasser's "people." In this way, Kureishi draws in the discourses of nationalism and patriotism and the commodification of "Englishness" with those of race and community, and attempts to deny any reductive reading. New York functions in direct counterpoint to London; metaphorically it reflects the trappings and the snares of fame and success but Karim still prefers his own "bitter, fractured country in turmoil" and the prospects of a part in a TV soap opera intending to tackle contemporary issues (259).

From Iain Chambers' "obscured" metropolis, to John Clement Ball's "semi-detached" metropolis, there are many ways of thinking about literary London. For Orwell, the place to look for "the germs of the future England" was "the arterial roads," in the suburbs or the "outskirts," the title of a 1981 play by Kureishi. In *The Buddha of Suburbia* Haroon declaims "There are many more things in heaven and earth, than you damn well dream of in Penge" (27). Kureishi is certainly not the first writer to satirize the suburbs: from George and Weedon Grossmith's classic comedy *The Diary of A Nobody* (1892), chronicling the absurd petty life of London clerk Charles Pooter, and H. G. Wells' *The New Machiavelli* (1910), to George Orwell's own *Coming Up For Air* (1939) and John Betjamen's Slough which "isn't fit for humans now," English writers have castigated the suburbs. They are a creative source of conflict and comedy, a backdrop where existence is sheltered but bland, a kind of manufactured monotony in which vacuous lives are lived out in what James Kunstler has called "the Geography of Nowhere." It is easy to laugh at the social enclaves where most Britons have grown up and since Kureishi believes that English values are suburban values, he is particularly acerbic about the stifling containment of suburban desires. People in Chislehurst would, Karim is convinced, "exchange their legs" for "velvet curtains, stereos, Martinis, electric lawnmowers, double glazing"(51). He compares his father's idyllic childhood in the exciting city of Bombay with his own dreary suburban sprawl of "gardens, lawns, greenhouses, sheds and curtained windows" (62).

Kureishi poses questions about the ways in which suburban living impacts on his characters. The suburbs are traditionally an "in-between" space — between city and country, and public and private lives — and so they function metaphorically in the novel as the liminal space Karim inhabits as he negotiates his way from adolescence to adulthood, and from margin to center. According to Alison Light, suburbia is typically "Janus-faced," not unlike Karim in his confusion over sexual and racial identity — or Haroon, a lapsed

Muslim commodifying himself for white suburbanites searching for the "inner room" as an Oriental-Hindu "Buddhist" guru. Haroon leaves his wife sitting at home in the suburbs watching television, a model of John Hartley's idea that female surburbanites are constructed through television, while he "buddhas off" beyond Bromley with Eva, whose primary goal is to "scour that suburban stigma" from her skin (134).

Suburbia sits at the nexus of a variety of contemporary forces: consumerism, lower middle-class complacency, political mobilization of voting districts, transport and traffic, and the green belt. It is hugely familiar and enduring and, for today's readers, often nostalgic and hackneyed. One is reminded that the word suburb owes much to expansion of work and leisure in the 1950s and some of Kureishi's descriptions are eerily reminiscent of the era, "scores of front rooms containing familiar strangers and televisions shining like dying lights" (74). Kureishi spends a lot of time delineating the suburbs. Bromley and Beckenham are filled with kids wearing velvet and satin and bright colors, "some were in bedspreads and curtains" (8); Chislehurst is "a lower middle-class equivalent of the theatre" (29) and, therefore, much more contradictory than the ubiquitous stereotypes would seem to allow. Obviously the suburbs have to be sufficiently banal for the protagonist to wish to escape them but some of the most surreal scenes take place in Karim's neighborhood. In suburbia, Karim undertakes an apprenticeship in how to be transgressive and Eva's successful career in interior design is initiated there. As Kureishi wryly states in "Finishing the Job," an essay describing a visit to Bromley ten years after moving out, "Look into the centre of the suburban soul and you see double-glazing. It was DIY they loved in Thatcherland . . . the concrete display of hard-earned cash." Fewer reviewers than one might expect have spent much time on how this particular item in the title's lexicon feeds the fantasy of self-renewal that underpins this novel. But many more have engaged with the images of Asians and the controversy that undergirds the representation of this particular group of British citizens.

IMAGES OF THE ASIAN FAMILY IN BRITAIN

In telling stories of individuals, Kureishi acknowledges the multifarious complexity of Asians' experiences in Britain. He strives to open up and to deconstruct popular misconceived images of British Asians. In *The Buddha of Suburbia* Kureishi creates families when this particular image of Asians is the most redolent, and frequently vilified in the popular press. A study published shortly before *Buddha* argues that the umbrella term "the Asian family" performs a "double conjuring trick." Within it "disappear the many types of Asian family structures, specific religions, cultures and migratory patterns, alongside the great variety of family life found here . . . a caricature is developed in opposition to an account of *the* British family which posits it as open and non-patriarchal." Sociologists Sallie Westwood and Parminder Bhachu describe this as a "convenient fiction" because it ignores what we have come to understand about the workings of power relations in *all* families. It also elides the fact that Asian families *are* British families and, as they point out, it underestimates the extent to which Asian families are a "major source of strength and resistance against the racism of British society."

The "popular" image of the Asian family involves tropes of the authoritarian patriarch, the unhappy arranged marriage, and the Asian woman as submissive victim of the family itself. These features would seem to characterize the family unit that is Anwar, Princess Jeeta, and Jamila in Kureishi's novel. They do not comprise the focal family but they, and the writer's representation of them, form the crux of the predicament of responsibility that Kureishi finds himself in vis-a-vis his critics. Kureishi obviously feels that he should engage with such a tenacious stereotype but this facet of *Buddha* is one with which even the most favorable reviewers of the novel have frequently felt uncomfortable — and endeavored to ignore. Neil Berry in the *London Review of Books* writes "in Karim's uncle Anwar, Jamila is faced with an obdurate Muslim father, bent on lining up an arranged marriage for her," exhibiting the kind of reviewers' shorthand that is only possible when the image of that particular confrontation is already clearly inscribed within the minds of the reading public. Berry does not engage with issues of representation though:

All this might well seem to justify claims that Hanif Kureishi trades in facile caricatures of Asians. But his quality as an observer of Asian mores becomes a less obtrusive issue when the narrative shifts from the suburbs to London itself.

Like Angela Carter in the *Guardian* and Hermione Lee in the *Independent*, Berry celebrates the novel's humorous ebullience. Lee does address the issue of representation, finally deciding, "perhaps Karim/Kureishi's gift is not for political heartsearching or answerability but for ruthless, farcical improvisation."

Kureishi presents the Anwar family as a foil for the Amirs and in so doing he also shows that not all families are the same. However, to dismiss the Anwars as nothing more than facile caricatures would be to miss the point. In Jamila and her mother we have two very strong women who are conscious of the roles assigned to them within a traditional working-class family unit, be the family black or white. I would argue that they choose to uphold a patriarchal structure that they know to be crumbling. Furthermore, it would be grossly inaccurate to see Jamila as an uncomplicated victim of her parents, when she is, in fact, given a great deal of freedom to pursue her own interests, in contrast to the stereotypical image that would have her at the parents' beck and call, dressed in salwar kameez, head bowed and acquiescent.

Jamila is a politicized character, presented in counterpoint to Karim who admits that: "compared to Jammie I was, as a militant, a real shaker and trembler. If people spat at me I practically thanked them for not making me chew the moss between the paving stones" (63). She stands up for her rights and is prepared to fight her aggressors: "once a greaser rode past us on an old bicycle and said, as if asking the time, 'Eat shit, Pakis'. Jammie sprinted through the traffic before throwing the bastard off his bike and tugging out some of his hair, like someone weeding an overgrown garden" (53). Jamila's political views can be located not only within the texts she reads, works by Simone de Beauvoir, Angela Davis, and George Jackson, but also in relation to political organizing against racism in the late 1970s, especially the campaigns launched by Black women's movements, Asian youth, and community groups. To delimit a reading of *Buddha*'s Asian women characters is to perpetuate and maintain a stereotypical hierarchy that Kureishi goes some way towards demolishing.

Readers may laugh at Kureishi's portrait of Ted, Jean's henpecked husband, and find little that is morally or politically awkward in that representation, but when it comes to the gentle mocking of his Asian characters there is sometimes a strong feeling of (misplaced) disquiet. Jamila is astute enough to acknowledge that "families aren't sacred" (55), but she also concedes that they have ways of asserting control. For example, her father attempts to rule his household with an iron fist, a fist that is directed at Jeeta until his daughter threatens to "cut off his hair with a carving knife" (58). But, with the end of physical violence, comes the birth of nonphysical violence and it is this latter form of warfare that Anwar directs at his wife and daughter to encourage them to bend to his will. In Anwar, Kureishi demonstrates that the "old ways" first generation immigrants are prone to cling to outside their country of birth are outmoded and redundant. Indeed, when seeking the "buddha's" advice on the potential arranged marriage Haroon sagely responds "We old Indians come to like this England less and less and we return to an imagined India" (74); it is this India of the imagination that drives Anwar, in belligerent patriarchy, into commencing his hunger strike. Anwar overlooks his own English "freedom" which includes "the prostitutes who hung around Hyde Park" whom "he loved" (25). Instead, by evoking Islam he represents himself as having a "fixed identity" that originates in his "motherland" and it is this that Kureishi deplores and satirizes.

For the author, one of the fundamental problems in British society is a hankering after a fixed, unbending, originary identity that takes little account of the various ethnic groups and communities that comprise contemporary Britain. In his creative representations Kureishi can be read as refuting any vestigial belief in transcendental racial or cultural categories. As he represents it, this is not the sole purview of whites but also of immigrants, especially those who espouse an uncritical orthodoxy. Karim reminds the reader "Like many Muslim men — beginning with the Prophet Mohammed himself, whose absolute statements, served up piping hot from God, inevitably gave rise to absolutism — Anwar thought he was right about everything. No doubt on any subject ever entered his head" (172). Such fixed views inevitably lead to conflict. Jamila operates strategically, endorsing an open and flexible stance — which, I would argue, leads her into "accepting" her father's choice of husband, Changez, in the knowledge that the marriage will operate on her terms, and be "a rebellion against rebellion, creative novelty itself" (82). In managing her situation in this way, Jamila prevents her father's death and curtails the violence directed at her mother. After Anwar's aborted hunger strike, Jeeta succeeds in making his life miserable (through food and silence) while, at the same time, taking control of the family business. Bilquis in *My Beautiful Laundrette* "bewitches" Nasser's mistress, while his daughter, Tanya, craves independence on her own terms and leaves the family fold. Amjad and Banoo's daughter, Amina in the play *Borderline*, enjoys a sexual relationship outside of marriage and joins a group of Asian activists against racism; Yasmin, in the same play, leaves the husband her family arranged for her.

Kureishi has always been interested in families and family relationships (as indicated by his comments on this topic in the interview that precedes this chapter). However, his focus is not limited to father-daughter relationships, as the discussion above might seem to suggest. Some of Kureishi's most interesting representations are father-son relationships. From *Borderline* in 1981 to his most recent novel *Gabriel's Gift* (2001), Kureishi has examined the complex ways in which fathers and sons interact. In *Borderline*, Haroon defends his father against charges that he only employs cheap immigrant labor in his restaurant, even though he ultimately escapes him and restaurant work by leaving for university. Gabriel does everything he can to save his father's relationship with his mother. Kureishi shows that children assume as much responsibility for parents as parents do for their offspring: Gabriel admires Rex, but more than that he respects him, even though he is reduced to living in a grubby bed-sit. Indeed, his son helps Rex find work and is ultimately responsible for reconciling his parents. Even Kureishi's most comic work is invested with scenes of respect and admiration across the generations. For example, Omar respects Papa, but aspires to follow Nasser as his role model in *My Beautiful Laundrette*; even though, superficially at least, Sammy doesn't much care for Rafi, he still respects and admires him in *Sammy and Rosie Get Laid*. Even in *My Son the Fanatic* in which most relationships collapse or are severed, the father preserves his love for his son, despite the son's blinkered disrespect being in stark contrast to the Islamic teachings he claims to have fully embraced. It is only in *London Kills Me* that the father-son relationship is shown to be beyond repair, but this is clearly the result of the father's absence.

In *The Buddha of Suburbia* the central relationship of Haroon and Karim dominates our understanding of the novel. Karim, growing up in Britain, has consistently been positioned as "Other" within his own society but this has not always been the case for first generation immigrants like Haroon. Haroon's generation either attempted to disregard a projected "negative identity" or learned their Otherness in Britain. Kureishi tells the stories of the father *and* of the son and differentiates between their experiences. Haroon has "lived in the West for most of my life, and I will die here, yet I remain to all intents and purposes an Indian man. I will never be anything but an Indian" (263). Whereas Karim describes himself as "an Englishman born and bred, almost. I am often considered to be a funny kind of Englishman, a new breed as it were, having emerged from two old histories. But I don't care — Englishman I am (though not proud of it)" (3). Kureishi explores the issues inherent in both these descriptions, through an examination of their father-son relationship.

From the outset the reader is aware of the link, or yoke, that binds the two characters. This is established during Haroon's yoga routine when he encourages his son to read from his favorite book, *Yoga for Women.* As Judith Misrahi-Barak explains, the term yoga derives from the Sanskrit root *yuj* which means to link, unite, or "to put under the same yoke." It also connotes: "the union, or even communion, between the different components of the human being — physical, mental and spiritual, and between the individual and the world." This establishing scene serves to unite the two characters before they embark on their escapade to Eva Kay's house, and functions, at the novel's outset, to designate the nature of their relationship. Their connection is based on the closeness of family rather than, as Kenneth Kaleta attests, "a typical adolescent power struggle" in which Haroon "orders" Karim help him practice his yoga. Each character has his own *particular* motives for attending Eva's soiree, but these motives overlap and intersect: father and son desire mother and son. And they each witness the other's "transgression," Haroon's extra marital lovemaking with Eva and Karim's homosexual masturbation of Charlie, which, in turn, cements their relationship beyond the filial with each sharing and protecting the other's "secret."

Adolescent Karim hopes that he is "going somewhere" and so partially mirrors his father who is going somewhere *else:* leaving his wife and children, his life as an employee in the Civil Service, and finally the suburbs. Concomitantly, Karim is taking leave of his mother and brother, his life as an adolescent, and the suburbs. It is no accident that Haroon tells his son that "we are growing up together" (22). The two utilize different but similar vehicles to escape their previous identities: Haroon becomes the "buddha" of suburbia and Karim takes to the stage as an actor. Haroon jettisons a career spent earning a pittance as a servant to Her Majesty's Government, where he knows that he will not be promoted ("The whites will never promote us. . . . Not an Indian while there is a white man left on the earth") but is expected to play the mimic man, taking orders and serving "his country" (27). However, it would be inaccurate to assume that mimicry cannot also be a form of subtle and potentially subversive power. As Jacques Lacan says:

Mimicry reveals something in so far as it is distinct from what might be called an itself that is behind. The effect of mimicry is camouflage. . . . It is not a question of harmonizing with the background, but against a mottled background, of becoming mottled — exactly like the technique of camouflage practiced in human warfare.

Throughout the course of his life in England, Haroon succeeds in leading a mottled existence, demonstrating the sublimation of his past, but the "itself that is behind" comes into focus during his "buddha" phase. No longer does he desire to be "less risibly conspicuous": "He was hissing his s's and exaggerating his Indian accent. He'd spent years trying to be more of an Englishman . . . and now he was putting it [Indianness] back in spadeloads" (21). Haroon frees himself of the identity that has been imposed upon him by his work and family, specifically Ted and Jean who think that it is "bad enough his being an Indian in the first place, without having an awkward name too. They'd called Dad Harry from the first time they'd met him" (33). The concept of mimicry is also applicable to Karim. In playing Kipling's Mowgli he finds an identity thrust upon him, precisely because Shadwell's conceptions of identity are predicated on essentialist notions. He asks Karim whether he speaks another language before ordering him to "put on" a false Indian accent along with his yellow scarf while smeared in a "shit-brown cream" (146), informing him that he has been "cast for *authenticity* and not for experience" (147; my italics). The majority of the white characters the reader encounters in this work have preconceived notions of identity, believing that as "foreigners" Haroon and Karim should act and behave in authentic ways. However, both characters turn the tables on those who would see them as "other" by subverting expectations: Haroon through his teaching and wisdom, which is initially seen as a performance ("Your father looks like a magician", 31), and Karim through, for example, adopting a Cockney accent in the middle of his representation of Mowgli.

Karim follows his father faithfully and learns from him, even though some of his teaching is rather unconventional. For example: "Dad taught me to flirt with everyone that I met, girls and boys alike, and I came to see charm, rather than courtesy or honesty, or even decency, as the primary social grace. And I even came to like people who were callous or vicious provided they were interesting" (7). Karim is also quick to acknowledge that the father presents his ethnicity as an element the individual may or may not choose to endorse:

I felt ashamed and incomplete at the same time, as if half of me were missing, and as if I'd been colluding with my enemies, those whites who wanted Indians to be like them. Partly I blamed Dad for this . . .
he wasn't proud of his past, but he wasn't unproud of it either; it just existed, and there wasn't any point in fetishizing it, as some liberals and Asians radicals liked to do. So if I wanted the additional personality bonus of an Indian past, I would have to create it. (213)

Karim sees identity as something one invents on the one hand and as something one may chose to inherit on the other. He only "partly" blames his father because he can see that in not pushing an identity on him, he refuses to act like those whites who position him in a particular way. Both characters adopt what Gayatri Spivak has called "strategic essentialism": performing ethnicity, in order to achieve their own ends without, in this case, causing too much damage to those around them. In the end Haroon and Karim adopt the same credo: "we must find an entirely new way of being alive" (32). This would seem to me to completely counter Kaleta's assertion that, "Karim is anxious to free himself from his father as part of his process of growing up: The son escapes his father's domination and asserts his independence."[6] Rather, Karim knows his life choices are inextricably bound up with the connection he has with his father.

LOOSENING THE IDEA OF EMPIRE: THE POLITICS

OF REPRESENTATION

Hanif Kureishi has referred to writers like himself as cultural trans-
lators and to writing about contemporary British communities as
involving "the psychological loosening of the idea of Empire." This
would immediately appear to locate his work in relation to postcolonial critic Homi Bhabha's discussions of cultural translation as
deriving from the hybridity of cultures, and of the process of representation undermining any pretence to "a holistic, organic identity."
Kureishi's comment also could be said to align him with Salman
Rushdie who in the essay "The New Empire Within Britain" explores dominant images of immigrants and their relation to institu-
tional racism, "in the new Empire, as in the old one, it seems our
masters are willing to use the tried and trusted strategies of divide-
and-rule." Rushdie has also discussed writers who offer what he calls
"stereoscopic vision" rather than "whole sight" in that they succeed
in seeing *between* and *across* cultures. Kureishi is a prime example
and he adjudges that one's identity has to be "some sort of alliance
between the way you see yourself and the way other people in the
world see you." Together, they allude to the kind of double consciousness or dual vision that black cultural critics and commentators from W. E. B. DuBois and Frantz Fanon to A. Sivanandan and
Henry Louis Gates Jr. have exposed and explored in writing about
issues of representation.

It is also possible to locate Kureishi's writing within contemporary debates about identity politics in a "dis-United Kingdom." He
has been asked repeatedly to state and explain his position and to
quantify it in the light of a changing Britain: "I'm an English writer,
a British writer, let's say, with an Indian background. And there's

going to be more and more of that in England." Interestingly, though, despite the (sometimes wary and often weary) self-definition required of him, it is also difficult to pin Kureishi down, to *quantify* his artistic intentions in the light of popular and critical reactions to his work. This is, I would argue, partly the result of what Kobena Mercer has called the structural predicament of the black artist and intellectual and partly due to Kureishi's flirtation with controversy, his willingness to grapple with issues that are at once populist *and* intellectualized. Todd Pruzan, in his *Washington Post* review of *Gabriel's Gift*, recently observed that "A spoonful of glam rock helps the politics go down" and, as this study of *The Buddha of Suburbia* shows, Kureishi is adept at tempering serious interrogation of Britain's flaws and fallacies with huge portions of satirical comedy, choosing the kinds of literary topics and making the kind of observations in the press that catch public attention.

In *Buddha* Karim has learned from his father that, with the empire exhausted, he should "never let the ex-colonialists see you on your knees" or to fail to make the most of any opportunities he may have (250). One is reminded of U.S. Secretary Dean Acheson's famous statement of 1962 that when Britain lost its Empire, it failed to find a new role. When Ian Jack ponders the subject he observes, "how odd we thought the periphery could shrink, and the centre stay unchanged." It is precisely in the interstices between the center and the periphery, and the past and the present, that Kureishi finds a new perspective that animates Karim's barreling progress through post-imperial Britain.

In Kureishi's writing, the politics of representation is inextricably linked to what is often a precarious membership of a British community, and by extension a multi cultural Europe.[7] This is not to say that Kureishi seeks to create a group identity that is "Asian" and "British"; rather, he illustrates the diverse forms of membership of any community. Membership of "the" Asian "community" in contemporary Britain ranges from that *necessary* to African Asian refugees fleeing Amin's Uganda or *encouraged* to leave Kenyatta's Kenya to that *negotiated* by first generation immigrants like Nasser and Hussein in *My Beautiful Laundrette* and Haroon in *The Buddha of Suburbia* to that *challenged* by Karim and Jamila in the same novel. Karim and Jamila are young Britons for whom identity politics is relational, an extension of the political and ideological times and tides within British society. They rail against the burgeoning right-wing movements of the late 1970s and Karim can be read against his younger brother Amar, or Allie, who hates "whingeing lefties" and "people who go on all the time about being black" and loves Italian clothes and soap operas (267–8).

An early essay by Paul Gilroy is particularly close in its identification of the intersection between class, race, and cultural identity to the issues that Kureishi explores. In "You can't fool the youths . . ." a contribution to a *Race and Class* special issue on the "riot"-torn Britain of 1981, Gilroy describes an enduring image of working-class Black communities from the 1970s on. In doing so he captures the stereotyping of young people like Karim and Jamila explored (or as some may say re-inscribed) by Kureishi:

the image of the respectable and hard-working first generation of black immigrants locked in struggle with their children, whose "identity crises" and precarious "between two cultures" impel them into deviant behaviour. Rejecting the parental culture whilst reproducing its pathological characteristics, these young people, whether of Asian or Afro-Caribbean origin, are presented as divorced from their parents' concerns. *This powerful stereotype unites self-proclaimed radical and openly racist theories of black life* (my emphasis).

This final sentence encapsulates the dilemma inherent in representing many of the characters in *Buddha* when that representation

can be tipped either way on the scales of political and moral responsibility. Kureishi has, it seems to me, often been judged according
to a political agenda of the 1970s that expressed the need to formu-
late positive images that would perform a public relations exercise
for the community to which the artist belonged. But he has simul-
taneously found himself judged according to the tenets of a 1980s
political agenda that sought to articulate raced subject positions in
ways that prove them to be both heterogeneous and sophisticated.
Kureishi has been caught between a rock and a hard place and he
expresses this anomalous position through Karim's dilemmas in *The
Buddha of Suburbia,* over his dramatic presentations of Changez
and Anwar and his rendition of Mowgli. Karim strikes a number of
poses and he takes on a number of roles but he always weighs his
experiences against his conscience or spiritual loneliness, and the
ways in which others act towards him or perceive him. It is only
very late in the novel that he moves beyond his childhood friend
Charlie, whom he has so revered and desired, and in an epiphany
of self realization is left "discovering myself through what I rejected"
(255). Many of the problems with which Karim grapples dramatize
quite complicated debates over representation.

Problems arise when a Black artist is straitjacketed into the formulaic series of expectations — when he or she suffers the burden of
representation. This containment leads to a desire to tell stories
other than the ones expected of a writer. Expectations that he will
carry the burden of representation have dogged Kureishi since his
earliest work, most particularly as a result of films that reached a
mass popular audience. Perminder Dhillon-Kashyap, in an otherwise thoughtfully argued piece, worries that in *My Beautiful Laundrette* Kureishi "has created a new victim, the white fascist — a
victim of economic circumstances who is being exploited by petty
bourgeois Asian businessmen." Dhillon-Kashyap is concerned about
the possibility of Kureishi perpetuating pernicious stereotypes. Ku-

reishi, though, is unafraid of employing problematic paradigms to politicized effect. He entitled his feature in *Time Out* on *My Beautiful Laundrette* "Dirty Washing" and, in portraying Omar as an Asian "underpants cleaner" in the film he challenges, both figuratively and literally, the unspoken imperative that has always been necessary in maintaining an unassailable imagined community of Englishmen: "that we should never discuss our differences in public: that we should always delay our criticism and do our dirty laundry in private." Kureishi provides an ironic twist on the idea since the clientele of the launderette are white British. It is they who wash their clothes publicly (as Nasser declares "There's money in muck. What is it the gorra Englishman always needs? Clean clothes!"), and Kureishi who takes the dirty laundry of the white British themselves as his subject matter.

Kureishi's rejoinder after the release of *My Beautiful Laundrette* was "the Asian community think that I'm perpetually throwing shit at them." He appears to remove himself from that community in this statement but rather than simplistically denying his own place within that community, he is questioning the idea of community itself. Kureishi refuses to see community in monolithic terms so that when critics maintain that his work is fragmentary and unstructured arguably they are perceiving Kureishi's artistic response to the "structure" of the Asian community (and of Britain) as *bricolage*; as an incredibly diverse, heterogeneous peoples yoked together under the political aegis of Asian or Black as a result of the Othering of their communities by white British institutions. Neither cultural nor national identity is organic but social institutions may operate hegemonically to make it appear so. Floya Anthias and Nira Yuval-Davis worry that "Britain" constructs members of minority cultures as a homogeneous group, which speaks with "a unified cultural voice." Taking the argument a step further, it becomes necessary to distinguish the "minority" voice from the "majority" culture in order for them to be seen as different. In this sense, the more distanced or alienated a community is from the center, the more "authentic" it is also seen to be. This is precisely the imagined construction of the community that Kureishi has been assessed from within and it is powerfully entrenched.

Gurinder Chadha, director of the short *I'm British But . . .* and the acclaimed *Bhaji on the Beach*, commented in 1989 that in her view for minority communities "having a British identity is not as important as having a cultural identity." She described making *I'm British But . . .* as a way of paying her dues to her *own* community, that is to say the Asian community in Britain. She assessed Kureishi as "quite isolated from the Asian side of himself. If there's one criticism of him, it's that he's used that side of him without real cultural integrity."[8] Chadha has fallen into the assumption that aligns a particular culture with a particular ethnic identity and reflects the continued allure of ethnic absolutes, an idea that Paul Gilroy, among others, rejects in *There Ain't No Black in the Union Jack* as a patent oversimplification of British experiences of raced identity.

Kureishi creates complex and contradictory hybridized citizens whose cultural identities are inextricably linked with class politics. He does not represent Asian peoples collectively or their communities as static; only if individuals that may be said to constitute an ethnically recognizable group are threatened and besieged do they consider that mass identity formation may serve a political and survivalist purpose. In *Buddha*, although British Asian culture is not presented as an ethnic absolute, Kureishi explores the ways in which it may be bound up with the projected negative identity that all citizens who are *not* white are subject to, as when Hairy Back calls Karim "a little coon":

"We don't like it," Hairy Back said. "However many niggers there are, we don't like it. We're with Enoch. If you put one of your black 'ands near my daughter I'll smash it with a 'ammer! With a 'ammer!"(40)

Kureishi succeeds in creating diverse British communities of which characters of Asian backgrounds are members. This may no longer seem new as we read successful novels by Salman Rushdie, Meera Syal, and more recently Zadie Smith, but Kureishi was the first to explode onto the scene and break into what remains an underdeveloped area of British fiction.

CONCLUSION

For Kureishi, writing is bound up with inescapable and exciting issues around performed identity and identity politics and is fraught with pitfalls and problems. In the 1980s when Kureishi began work on *Buddha* this very predicament contributed to his vibrant engagement with issues of representation, including "Englishness." Kureishi is not constrained by any expectations that may be attributed to him and *The Buddha of Suburbia* revitalizes and broadens definitions of self and Englishness. Kureishi asserts his authorial control over any "cultural" responsibility he may be deemed to have and has said on many occasions that he really does not care what other people may want him to write. His apparently cynical hardiness should not distract our attention from what is also a thoughtful, thoroughgoing analysis of his writerly position in Britain. Even in the same interview in which he derides those who assume what his appropriate subject matter may be, he confides:

You would flatter yourself if you thought you could change things by a film or a play or whatever, but perhaps you can contribute to a climate of ideas.

It may be that you write a film about Asians or gay people . . . people may see this as being a normal part of everyday life and not a sort of freak show on the margins. It is important to ask questions about how we live sexually, how we live racially, what our relations are with each other emotionally. Asking these questions seems to me to be the things artists can do rather than change society in any specific way.

Kureishi asks these kinds of questions in *Buddha* and he underpins each question with a recognition of how class politics affects sexual and interracial relationships and the ways that each dovetail into definitions of British democracy.[9] *The Buddha of Suburbia* is a larger book than its immediate plot and preoccupations would imply. While it is specific to its 1970s South England setting, it opens out onto a vista of two continents, and explores pop and youth culture across the disappearing Sixties, the rough and ready Seventies and nods wryly towards the yuppified Eighties. Kureishi creates a perfect match between setting and subject and in Karim, he fashions a persona who cuts a swathe through a series of poignant and comic situations. Though ironic he is never scathing about his young protagonist's hopes and ambitions, mistakes or failures. The novel was and still is a huge critical, commercial, and popular success.

3

The Novel's Reception

Hanif Kureishi's reputation as a spiky writer ensured that the publication of *The Buddha of Suburbia* would become the subject of considerable press coverage. But even Kureishi may well have been surprised to see the number of column inches reviewers devoted to his first novel. Two of the first reviewers off the blocks were the acclaimed novelist Angela Carter and the well-known literary critic Hermione Lee. Carter opens her review with "The narrator . . . is a child of Empire" but quickly unsettles any expectations of Raj revivalism by claiming that *The Buddha of Suburbia* may be "the first novel in what I trust will be a rapidly growing and influential genre, the novel designed on purpose to exclude itself from the Booker short list."[10] In this way, the novel was immediately singled out in the British press as brave and controversial. Readers have continued to be drawn to Kureishi for these reasons down the years since he is always sardonic and often "taboo-busting."

Reviewers of his first novel have tended to focus, to varying degrees, on a very few key areas. Firstly, Kureishi's literary antecedents. For example, Hermione Lee asserts that Kureishi's first novel is reminiscent of a series of distinct literary "models": "This garru-

lous, confiding voice, full of 'can you believes' and 'I'm not kid-
dings', owes a lot to America: to *The Catcher in the Rye*, to Saul
Bellow's Augie March . . . to Nathanael West's greenhorn astray in
the nightmare world of *A Cool Million*, and to the black picaresque
heroes of Richard Wright, James Baldwin and Ralph Ellison." The
American connection reflects the reading of his protagonist, Karim
who returns to America of the 1950s and 1960s in his reading
patterns, following his cousin Jamila's lead. More usually, a significant number of reviewers, as well as Kureishi himself, have been
quick to point out how very English the novel feels. In an article
for the *Guardian*, Frank Kermode argues that Kureishi's fiction is
reminiscent of H. G. Wells' work. Wells, a sharp social critic who
created aspiring members of the middle classes in *Kipps* (1905) and
The History of Mr. Polly (1910), was, like Kureishi, born in Bromley.
Kermode elucidates his position by setting up a detailed example by
which to compare the two writers: "Wells observed the struggles and
antics of an underclass in search of personal and social fulfillment,
and wrote about suburban drolls, mild grotesques, in what we think
of as a quasi-Dickensian way. Kureishi thinks of his own kind of
writing as in the tradition of the English comic novel, mentioning
not only Wells but Angus Wilson and Kingsley Amis as varied
representatives of that genre."[11] The underclass to which Kermode
alludes is represented in *Buddha* by British Asian characters; Kureishi effects a shift in our understanding of the stock characters the
English novel form generally encompasses. The "suburban drolls"
he creates in 1990 are often members of a minority "outsider"
population, embarking on the same search for personal and social
fulfillment that has energized more "traditional" English writing.

The second area of interest, like the first, reflects the reviewers'
task of locating the novel in terms of genre as well as literary
influences. Reviewers wonder whether *The Buddha of Suburbia*
may safely be labelled a comic novel, and left at that. Or, is it really

an urban tragedy, or a melodrama, or a treatise on race relations? It would be hard to contest the appellation of comic novel but critics have also recognized all of the aforementioned elements in their reviews. For Hermione Lee, *Buddha* is "one of the sharpest satires on race relations in this country" and Michiko Kakutani follows suit, stating in the *New York Times* that it is at once "a traditional comedy of manners" *and* "a scathing satire on race relations in Britain." However, Kakutani is not oblivious to the fact that life in Britain involves Asians finding themselves positioned as victims of white oppression. She compares Kureishi to V. S. Naipaul in this regard, "he has a gift for locating the hypocrisies that inform relationships between the white and nonwhite worlds, and absolutely no misgivings about exposing those hypocrisies on both sides. Patronizing white liberals, scheming third world hustlers, sycophantic immigrants and guilty ex-colonialists: all are depicted in uncompromisingly satiric terms." Kureishi has frequently bemoaned the fact that, traditionally, the British novel excludes precisely these sorts of topics, "Politics, the lives of immigrants, the changes in British society — and also pop culture, which isn't just a trivial sideshow."

A predictable area of focus is the intersection between British "race relations" and the author's biography, that is to say, Kureishi's heritage as a mixed race writer in contemporary Britain. Although critics do not stretch to examine this facet of his work in critical terms, they do acknowledge concepts like the politics of identity and hybridity as discussed earlier in this study. For example, Paul Bailey's review in the *Sunday Times* takes account of cultural hybridity without actually exploring how it functions: "the picture it offers of an Indian-English way of life in an always recognisable London . . . is of special interest." More typically, critics refer to cultural hybridity in order to reassure readers that this facet of the novel does not fix it as "minority interest", as demonstrated by M. G. Lord's comments in *Newsday*, "Like Kureishi, Karim . . . is an

Anglo-Asian.... But he is also a universal type." This denial of specificity can be annoying. At its worst, "universal" has become a coded way of expressing that with which white westerners can empathize so that ethnic specifics are rendered superficial. In an essay in *To Criticize the Critic*, T. S. Eliot, though frequently cited by those who espouse monocultural ideas of cultural identity, says "I doubt whether a poet or novelist can be universal without being local too" and he recognizes that writers may convey the local archetypally "in the mythology of men everywhere." Hermione Lee is perhaps the most perceptive reviewer on this topic when she acknowledges: "Kureishi's work ... centres on an Anglo-Asian 'in-betweener's' love-hatred of Britain," though she fails to elaborate on the role of the in-betweener in contemporary British society. The most cogent of reviewers in this context is Robin Epstein, writing in the *Courier Journal*, who believes that *The Buddha of Suburbia* "rightly undermines the impression some might have mistakenly picked up about British Muslims from the calls for the head of Salman Rushdie.... They are far from being a fundamentalist monolith of book burners." This reviewer recognizes the heterogeneity of British-Asians. However, the focus on his mixed-race identity is something that has come to haunt Kureishi: in representing him as both "insider" and "outsider," he has been called upon to speak for and to represent both communities and, sometimes, as a result, he has become a target for both groups.

Commentary on the novel's setting takes up quite a substantial part of many reviews. Kureishi has famously described himself as a Londoner and his first novel is as much about London as it is about the suburbs. However, not all reviewers believe that the second part of the novel (the London section) is as well-crafted as the first. Anthony Appiah in the *New York Times* calls *Buddha* an "extremely funny" read and its characters "both flawed and appealing." But he is also concerned that the novel "dragged" towards the end after a "brilliant beginning." Ian Buruma compartmentalizes the novel in this way, stating in the *New Republic* that "the inner-city half of the book is less good than the suburban part." Richard Eder speaks of an "awkward and disappointing second half" in which the story "turns thin and cartoonish." Eder sees *Buddha* as a developmental stage in Kureishi's writing career, moving out from the screenplays to a novel about "England and her Third World." Reading past what is unhelpful, out-moded, and inappropriate in Eder's terminology, he basically contends that there are two Londons. One is "London as idea," a city of stereotypes endorsed by the heritage industry and by Eder himself: commuters in bowler hats, pearly queens, Big Ben, the changing of the guard at Buckingham Palace. Eschewing economics, Eder believes these features encourage immigrants and the consequent creation of a second London of mosques and Caribbean markets. Eder's is an awkwardly expressed review but it goes some way towards conveying Kureishi's success in weaving together a London that otherwise seems to be "terminally fragmented" in British fiction, where second-generation immigrants try "to cope with being English" and the (white) English seem to have "lost any real identity of their own."[12] In a similar vein, Larry Fineberg asserts the novel is at its most focused when it "concentrates on the rich and jumbled assortment of England's Asian and black population." The focus on alterity tends to concentrate on British Asians as part of a national imaginary rather than actual British citizens, with reviewers deliberately avoiding talk of "race" by covering it over in discussions of ways of "belonging" to the British nation. One is sadly reminded of Paul Gilroy's observations that what is generally called "new racism" operates across left and right political distinctions when some reviewers tangle themselves in knots and fail to re-orient traditional ideas of "nation" or "Englishness."

An aspect of the novel that deserved more attention is cross-generational relationships and, most specifically, Karim's relationship with his father, as Felix Jimenez suggests in *The Nation*. It is a relationship Kureishi has spoken of openly and described as formative in a number of interviews. Recently, discussing his latest book, *Gabriel's Gift*, in a variety of fora, Kureishi confided he has always been interested in the father-son relationship. Jimenez traces what he sees as Karim's "unbearable fascination with phallic phantoms" back to Cat Stevens: "although musical references pop up throughout the book — everything from Nat King Cole to the Rolling Stones to Pete Townsend — the only song that really comes to one's mind is Stevens' syrupy 'Father and Son.' " This song, Jiminez contends, epitomizes their relationship: "Karim's politics are every bit as suburban as his father's, he just punks it out differently."

Not all reviews of *Buddha* have been positive. Novelist Bharati Mukherjee, while accepting that Kureishi is an "enormous talent" and ranking him alongside Salman Rushdie and Kazuo Ishiguro in his ability to encourage readers to rethink what "Englishness" means, is left feeling that *Buddha* is "profoundly unsatisfying." She fears it lacks focus and narrative momentum. Her view is determined by her expectations that there should have been a thoroughgoing analysis of Haroon, rather than Karim, a "smug, opportunistic, hyper-sensual, self-consciously charming, cruel adolescent." One can only imagine she feels he is too close to her own protagonist Jasmine in the eponymous novel of 1989. Mukherjee avers that Kureishi's *bildungsroman* lacks "emotional and moral resonance," the kind of criticism that has been directed at her own fiction. Like Fineberg, who contends that Karim is a tabula rasa, she feels Karim "never quite comes alive and is too often a vehicle for the author's opinions," one of the problems that surfaces for reviewers is that a novel based on first person narration is expected to conform to a socio-realist context. It would seem such criticisms fail to recognize the general literary consensus that a character's consciousness is a construction rather than a stable "self": "a locus of relationships rather than an ego in the older sense," as Fredric Jameson summarized as long ago as the early 1970s.

Mukherjee, it seems to me, wishes that Kureishi had written a different book; namely one that explored "national anxieties about cultural mongrelization"—like *Jasmine,* in which her immigrant protagonist plays out a series of different roles as she flirts with her new American identity. Sigificantly, though, Mukherjee is one of the few reviewers to comment specifically on Jamila, finding her a "truly admirable character." Only Angela Carter praises all of Kureishi's female characters: "He can't find a bad word to say about women . . . which is a lovely thing in this period of fashionable misogyny." Kureishi finds avid supporters easily as often as he is excoriated by reviewers who balk at his supposedly controversial views. In Carter and Mukherjee, Kureishi's first novel held the attention of two leading contemporary writers on both sides of the Atlantic.

One of the qualities for which *The Buddha of Suburbia* has been consistently applauded is its evocative period detail. Fineberg adjudges a "mood and time is adeptly evoked without sentimentality" and Robin Epstein goes even further and suggests that Kureishi has a "wry appreciation . . . of fashion, literature, music, politics and spirituality." This quality is something that Kureishi consciously aimed for in depicting a time and place as precisely as possible without romanticizing either aspect. When reviewers think he fails, they tend to overbalance towards the political right wing, like *The Economist's* unnamed reviewer who believes that "politics weakens . . . Kureishi's touch—as was apparent in his didactic and dismal second film, *Sammy and Rosie Get Laid.*" The reviewer pursues the point like a dog with a bone: "certain classes of people, the Rich and the Establishment, are Bad. Writing about these . . . Kureishi loses his sense of subtlety. But then he has also lost his peculiar vantage point; that of an outsider who is in a minority." This oddly tautological review traps Kureishi in a double bind: he is and is not an "outsider," or "British," or "political," in the "right" kind of didactic ways. Dependence on labels hampers some reviewers from reading and enjoying fiction. In the same review, Adewale Maja-Pearce's novel *How Many Miles to Babylon* is considered and the pitfalls of reading fiction as sociology become even more clear. Maja-Pearce is castigated for writing about "issues" when "what white readers need" is "to be able to get under the skin of somebody who is living with the problems." It is, of course, reductive to see fiction by black writers as potential self-help manuals for white readers.

Many adjectives have been used to describe *The Buddha of Suburbia*: "rich and Rabelaisian" (Fineberg); "penetrating" (Mukherjee); "witty and exhilarating" (Eder). For Kit Reed and the vast majority of reviewers and readers of the novel, "Traveling with Karim is a little like taking a guided tour in which the guide has been replaced by an attractive, large child who's fun to be with but easily distracted by strains of music and flashes of light and color. You may miss one or two major monuments as he whisks you from place to place, but traveling with him is a pleasure." I am certain that this is indeed the case since more than 600,000 people have bought the novel in 25 different languages[13] in order to experience the pleasure of traveling with Karim Amir.

The Television Adaptation

The adaptation of *The Buddha of Suburbia* was arguably Kureishi's biggest screen success since *My Beautiful Laundrette.* Kureishi really came to public prominence as the screenwriter of that highly successful film. So it is unsurprising that he agreed to adapt *The Buddha of Suburbia* for the screen. *My Beautiful Laundrette* is the story of two young men in Margaret Thatcher's Britain. Omar, who is Asian, and Johnny, who is white, embody Thatcher's call for entrepreneurism. In fact, Kureishi believes that the primary thing they have in common is "the desire to be rich . . . what they also want, which is one of the West's other projects, is to flaunt and demonstrate to others their wealth and prosperity."[14] At the same time, their homosexual relationship defies the kind of homophobia that gave rise to Clause 28 in 1988.[15] The film was a breakthrough success for the newly formed Channel 4, which was commissioning films by young writers and directors.

Kureishi's first film — like his first novel — has an exuberant energy through which it challenges fixed assumptions about the British Asian community and stereotypes of Asians as duty-bound, quiescent figures who long for a far-off homeland. Instead, the film shows characters clearly carving out a place for themselves in England; the Asians are not only local shopkeepers but also important business entrepreneurs. Significantly, it also depicts Asians as sexual beings, with sexual appetites (Nasser's comforting yet erotic affair with Rachel; Tania's sexual awakening and appreciation of the sensuality of her own body, and the central homosexual relationship of Omar and Johnny). The phenomenal success of the film, I think, rests in its elevation *and* debunking of themes of racial and sexual identity, transforming them into politically exciting comedy. In this, *My Beautiful Laundrette* is a pertinent forerunner of the novel: critically, *Buddha* stirred up the same kinds of battling reviewers. Max Davidson in "There's More to *The Buddha of Suburbia* than Naked Flesh" got to the heart of the debate pretty quickly:

The integrity of the drama was so striking that it was almost as if its creator Hanif Kureishi was taking the mickey out of the people who want to jump on the bandwagon and label him a pornographer. . . . The people who haven't grown up are the armchair censors who take fright at the sight of a naked bottom and cry foul before they have thought what it is they are objecting to. It is the context, always the context, that matters; and anyone who has watched this series will attest that it has taken a serious, rounded look at the strains of adolescence.

Of course not all viewers are ever happy. In the United States *My Beautiful Laundrette* was attacked by some members of the South Asian community on its release, as Kureishi describes in the interview that prefaces this study. But for each dispararging comment there is a corresponding note of praise. Stuart Hall describes the film as:

one of the most riveting and important films produced by a black writer in recent years and precisely for the reason that made it so controversial: its refusal to represent the black experience in Britain as monolithic, self contained, sexually stabilized . . . always and only "positive."

Examining the reception of *My Beautiful Laundrette* for a moment offers a wider context in which to understand the crucible of anxieties around race, sex, and class against which Kureishi has been judged. Kureishi's film and TV work has proved popular with a mass audience and this in itself gives rise to debates over commercial versus artistic success. June Givanni cites *My Beautiful Laundrette* together with Spike Lee's *She's Gotta Have It* as examples of the very few "relatively low-budget" feature films that have successfully " 'crossed over' from small art-house audiences to achieve commercial success in high street cinemas." British film critic Judith Williamson points out that those critics who sneer at *My Beautiful Laundrette* do so precisely because it proved so popular with audiences.

According to Kenneth Kaleta, Kureishi was initially reluctant to adapt *The Buddha of Suburbia* for the screen and only agreed to the project after several aborted attempts at adaptation resulted in bowdlerized versions of the text with deletions or additions he could not approve. In the end, Kureishi co-scripted with Roger Michell (*Notting Hill, Persuasion, Titanic Town*). At one point the BBC shelved plans to make a TV mini-series when they decided the book was too subversive and its sexual and political content might offend British licence-payers. In the period in which such discussions took place, in 1992, there appeared a rather idiotic piece of reporting when the *Daily Mail*'s Baz Bamigboye asserted that: "Much of the book is about Karim's bizarre sexual exploits, but the tome also deals with Karim's father . . . and various relatives. It is their rumblings about the state of Britain and exactly what should be done with the Conservative Government, which have caused concern." One imagines Bamigboye hadn't actually read the book, or that he failed to grasp the fact that it has less to do with a political party that wasn't in power in the period the novel took as its primary setting, and more to do with the spirited thrill-seeking of the hedonistic 1960s as they mediated into the nervous and more complicated 1970s. When the BBC decided to go ahead with the project, miniseries' producer Kevin Loader (*Captain Corelli's Mandolin*) remembers that the Corporation was "very supportive of us. We had one meeting as a team before we shot anything and agreed the number of four-letter words we could have. If you want to use 'fuck' on the television, it has to be cleared at the highest level. Our first draft of the scripts, I think, had fifty-three 'fucks' in it, and it was then, and it still is, very difficult to put these in home-grown products."

The British press had a field day when the 2.9 million pound adaptation of *The Buddha of Suburbia* was first screened in November 1993 on BBC2 as a four-part mini-series and was watched by some 5 million viewers. A number of blinkered, childish, and prudish observations were played out in the right-wing press. Lester Middlehurst of the *Daily Mail* criticized the BBC's pre-transmission warning about the program's content, calling it an "extraordinarily-worded voice-over." The voice-over itself is clear and alerts viewers to expect: "An unrestrained initiation into the excesses of the Seventies now on BBC2. Karim launches himself into the London scene and a variety of new experiences. There is strong language and explicit sex. Hey man, it's *The Buddha of Suburbia*." This is a fairly standard warning, and the program was transmitted after the watershed so minors should not have been watching without parental consent. Nevertheless, in his report of Thursday, November 18, 1993, the day after the third episode — containing full-frontal nudity and an orgy-scene — Lester Middlehurst was only one of the *Mail*'s commentators to be featured in a way that leans toward the outlandish. Each reviewer's comment is prefaced by whether he or she is single, married, or a parent, as if these "credentials" matter in this case. For example, Graham Turner, "married with three children," calls the adaptation "seedy, sordid, violent and brutalizing" and he "fear(s) for the mental health of those able to sit through it" (one wonders, then, whether he actually watched the *whole* episode, or whether he has special powers that protect his own mental health). Turner goes on to castigate *Buddha* as a "degrading offering" and to berate the BBC: "who is directing its affairs to allow the transmission of such foulness? Sadly, it is not untypical of the diet which it increasingly serves up." Marcus Berkmann ("single"), on the other hand, worries that "arguments about supposedly gratuitous sex should undermine such a clever, amusing and acutely observed series." But Mary Keeny ("married with two children") echoes Turner (of course) with, "It depressed me profoundly . . . the BBC once stood for culture, decency, dignity. And now, here it is portraying the sex act explicitly." She embraces the kind of rhetoric that finds Kureishi at the center of a watershed in British politics when she goes on to predict that, "One day the ordinary people will rebel against all this—either by voting for some extremely reactionary force or, even better, by turning their tellies over to something beautiful and sublime." Christopher Dunkley in "Up With Sex, Down With Violence" published the same week in the *Financial Times* enters the reviewing circle with a sensible observation that "attitudes to many subjects—Asians, contemporary music, mysticism—have been represented and variously parodied, ridiculed or attacked, and it would be odd, given the time and attention that so many people devote to it, if sex were to be left out." And one other reviewer from the *Daily Mail*, without marital designation, asserts "There was no way . . . that sex could have been avoided. The adaptation . . . was less—how can I put it?—action-packed than the novel, but it was unapologetic in its candor." Lynne Truss of the London *Times* is ecstatic: "Never has a novel waltzed so effortlessly on to the screen. The direction of Roger Michell is deft and humourous, the David Bowie soundtrack is an inspiration, and the casting is superb from Roshan Seth's embarrassingly emotional Haroon . . . to Vicky Murdock as the eager new girlfriend Helen."

The television series starred those actors already associated with earlier Kureishi or Kureishi/Frears film productions: Roshan Seth (*My Beautiful Laundrette, Gandhi, Mississippi Masala, A Passage to India, Indiana Jones and the Temple of Doom*) as Haroon; Naveen Andrews (*Wild West, The English Patient, My Own Country*) as Karim; Steven Mackintosh (*London Kills Me, Lock, Stock and Two Smoking Barrels, Land Girls, Prick Up Your Ears*) as Charlie; alongside Brenda Blethyn (*Little Voice, Secrets and Lies, Saving Grace, Girl's Night*) as Margaret; Susan Fleetwood (*Heat and Dust, The Krays*) as Eva; Nisha Nalyar as Jamila and Harish Patel (*My Son the Fanatic, Essence*) as Changez. Kureishi and Mitchell stayed loyal to the book but the screen adaptation is no less successful as a result.[16] Indeed, the TV adaptation brings the characters to life for those who have read the book and for those who read it as a result of watching the mini-series. As Kureishi himself admits in the interview for this book, the adaptation makes us see the actors in our mind's eye and we may well find that "the text is mediated though them. The actors have become superimposed on the text." For example, an accomplished actor like Roshan Seth can even alter the way in which a character is understood, as in the case of the *Daily Telegraph*'s reviewer: "Roshan Seth was surprisingly sympathetic as his Buddhist father. In the book, this character comes across as an amiable charlatan, but here his sincerity was impressive and his moments of forced uxoriousness, appeasing his tight-lipped wife, were strangely affecting."

Of course, one factor that is lost in the screen version, as Kureishi also states in the interview in chapter one, is the first person narration. Traditionally, we understand first person narratives—the "I" as protagonist—to situate a character at the center of the narrative who conveys events and experiences in his words and from his point-of-view. This type of narrative is also called homodiegetic narration, and this term often applies in discussions of television productions, where the narrator is a character in his own story. One of the main problems with homodiegetic narration is that the narrator cannot know everything; he is necessarily restricted to reporting only those events for which he is present, or interpreting what other characters may be thinking or feeling. *The Buddha of Suburbia* is semi-autobiographical, and Kureishi has often indicated that we should not assume an easy equation between self and story :

The Buddha was kind of autobiographical but it was revved up autobiography. One's childhood is mostly composed of very long tedious stretches when you mostly sit around wishing that exciting things would happen. In a book you put the exciting things one after another. When you read the book you think "wow this guy had a really good time down there in the suburbs." The relation between autobiography and your writing is a complicated one. . . . It came out of my experience in that sense, but it's not a direct one-on-one thing where something happens and you go and write it down. It's not like that . . . You mix all that stuff up together and then you get a good chapter.

In the case of the book's adaptation for television, the scriptwriters dispensed with first person narration. But, since the novel was conceived as a *bildungsroman* or rites of passage movement from adolescence to adulthood, they maintain a limited number of voice-overs. In an interview with Kaleta, Roger Michell acknowledges some of the difficulties they faced when adapting the novel, in particular, Karim who is "a prose character." On film Michell believes he becomes "more human." This is typically an audience response to realistic camerawork, continuity editing and the whole package that constitutes the conventions of classical narrative cinema. In this case, it is reinforced by reviewer Maureen Paton who found "What sometimes seemed slightly outlandish in the book, when filtered through narrator Karim's jaundiced schoolboy caricatures, has been triumphantly brought to life by director Roger Michell's exuberantly funny production of this affectionate satire." Predictably enough, not all critics preferred the screen representation of Karim. Elaine Paterson complains that although:

Like many teenagers the character is vain, arrogant and self-centred. In the novel these shortcomings are redeemed by the humour, honesty, and unerring sense of irony with which Karim homes in on the ludicrous elements of the '70s culture. The detachment that made Karim such an unusually objective narrator in the novel makes for a rather unengaging character on the screen. Television can't put us into his mind and whereas Karim is at the heart of the novel, in the TV version he's in danger of being swamped by the many outlandish people around him. We're not looking at them through his eyes, we're looking at him and them from the outside.

Most notably, the TV series successfully captures the atmosphere of the 1970s; the mise-en-scene is full of cultural and period markers. This is one aspect of the mini-series that, according to Kureishi, would be very difficult for the BBC to get wrong since it has a history of making quality "period" dramas, "I think the Beeb did it really well. They're good at costume drama." While one usually thinks of adaptations of classic nineteenth-century novels like those by Jane Austen, or Charles Dickens or George Eliot, the idea of *The Buddha of Suburbia* as "period drama" helps us to understand the critical approval it won—here from Peter Paterson in the *Daily Mail—specifically* for its recreation of the 1970s: "Roger Michell's direction was fast paced and attentive to all the necessary Seventies' detail. And the photography by John McGlashan, was a hymn to the Betjamenesque splendors of South London domestic architecture." One is reminded that when Kureishi was first interviewed on television on the publication of the novel, *Rear Window* and *The Late Show* included dramatized segments with "period" clothing, music, and scenes from TV, to create a sense of the 1970s. Similarly, Bowie's composition of an original soundtrack—with tracks including "Sex And The Church," "South Horizon," "Bleed Like Craze, Dad" and "Buddha Of Suburbia"—extrapolates on the novel and expands on it. Bowie has said "the narrative & 70's memories provid(ed) a textural backdrop in my imagination that manifested as a truly exciting work situation. In short, I took the TV play motifs and reconstructed them completely except, that is, for the theme song." [17]

The importance of historical and textual accuracy cannot be overstated, especially when the period under consideration and the novel are so very recent. The BBC decided to devote four hours to the program. The end result won the approval of the author and his mother: "It was a kind of period piece by the time it was finally made. . . . The BBC are very good at the wallpaper and the carpets. My mum said 'Cor, it's just like our 'ouse isn't it'. Which it was." Though tongue-in-cheek, Kureishi's comment captures the kind of empathy and identification that made for the dramatization's success. In one of the early scenes, where Karim is getting ready to leave with his father on their first journey to Eva's, his bedroom is conveyed as a veritable treasure trove of 1970s memorabilia. The walls are adorned with posters, there are piles of books including Jack Kerouac's cult hit *On the Road*, essays by James Baldwin, a Beatle's Sgt. Pepper's cut out, more piles of fashionable clothing of the era, and—in the middle of it all—Karim impersonating John Travolta's bedroom scene from *Saturday Night Fever* (1977). He dresses in time to Marc Bolan, the glam rocker of the 1970s, singing "Get it On," a song so suggestive it was re-titled "Bang A Gong" in the United States. Interestingly, in this scene Karim is the central focus and the audience takes on the role that is usually assigned to his character, namely that of voyeur. We watch in fascination and horror his selection and rejection of the evening's attire and witness the adolescent pamper himself with talcum powder in anticipation for his "outing." Indeed, this bedroom scene is so reminiscent of the classic scene from *Saturday Night Fever* that it might be viewed as a parody of the earlier movie. However, what shifts it beyond parody is the way that the mise-en-scene packages Karim for viewer consumption. In the novel Kureishi presents less than a page of description of Karim's preparations for the evening's excursion, yet on the TV the camera's gaze takes over: the camera caresses the young man and serves to establish Karim's difference and exoticism (there is no first person narration to tell the viewer that he is "an Englishman born and bred, almost").

Karim becomes the primary object of the viewer's gaze and in this way becomes caught up in his preparation for launching himself into unchartered territory "out there." His identity is particularized as a hybrid embodiment of two cultures in this sequence, as further reinforced when Karim makes his grand exit: dressed in tight, crushed velvet flared trousers, platform shoes, a flower-patterned shirt, and a suede jacket topped with a multi-colored scarf that acts as a bandana to hold down his long unruly hair. All this prompts his father simply to raise an eyebrow before turning away and his mother to exclaim: "Don't show us up, Karim. You look like Danny La Rue." For the viewer, Karim may well be a 1970s fashion victim but many viewers will recognize themselves, if not in his clothes, then certainly in the statement of (youth-sanctioned) "individuality" that the clothes are supposed to signify. Indeed, the stereotyped image of many Asian young men in the 1970s was precisely one that embodied them in Karim's extravagant "eastern" attire, as his father recognizes. For the older viewer accustomed to weekend television variety shows, Margaret's reference to the flamboyant Danny La Rue will, no doubt have some resonance. However, these visual cues have a more sinister meaning for Kureishi and that is the suburbanite desire for conformity, anything to stop the twitching of the neighbours' curtains and their condemning this mixed-race family to being somehow-less-than-normal. Danny La Rue was, of course, a hugely successful drag artiste and the hidden subtext of Margaret's comments is a concern for her son's sexuality, as displayed, she fears, in his attire. Again, the novel reinforces what the screen adaptation misses; the first person narration informing the reader that Karim is looking for sexual action of any kind, which culminates in his masturbating of his friend and soon-to-be stepbrother, Charlie. (Although he isn't looking for sexual action with a Great Dane even though he gets it in one memorable, visually comic scene.)

In the main, what the TV adaptation captures visually is that which Karim is attempting to subvert: the stale rigidity of the suburbs, that hinterland that would later be the heartland of Margaret Thatcher's Conservatism. This irony is not lost on the viewing public who, perhaps, do not hold out quite so much hope and optimism as Karim at the end of the series: with hindsight viewers in the 1990s know that the Conservative election victory did not herald an era of growth and progressive values; rather, it was a time of stultification and declension best embodied by the very suburbs Karim seeks to escape and that his yuppie younger brother so unquestioningly endorses. In his introduction to the 1992 collection, *London Kills Me: Three Screenplays and Four Essays*, Kureishi contends that Margaret Thatcher and the conservatives:

were afraid of anyone who saw Britain as a racially mixed run-down, painfully class-ridden place. For their fantasy was of a powerful, industrially strong country with a central homogeneous, consensual culture. There necessarily would be hinterlands, marginals, freaks, perverts, beggars, one-parent families, and dissidents but these didn't matter. There could be no other versions of reality escaping into the world, poisoning the purity of their vision.

What Kureishi has to say in 1992, the period in which he was working on the adaptation of *Buddha*, about Thatcher and her government might still apply to certain anxious members of the Asian community. After the final episode of *Buddha* was screened, Tessa Boase reported in the *Daily Telegraph* the following response from a London-based Asian town councilor: "That series has done untold damage to the British perception of Asians living in this country. The older generation has been shown to be narrow minded and old fashioned, and the younger generation outrageously rebellious and offensively promiscuous. There is no middle ground. What is worse, people are applying these caricatures to Asians in the Nineties. Things are not so extreme." Kureishi will not be worried by this reaction, nor, indeed, by the reactions of any of the journalists mentioned above. After all, he once said that the poll tax riots were "terrific" and, despite the cliché, any publicity is good publicity. He even attacked the BBC over potential cuts to *Buddha*, calling members of the Corporation "a bunch of nervous Nellies." One can only guess at his reaction to the American television executives who refused to buy the series on account of its sexual themes. As Nicholas Hellen wrote in the *Evening Standard*, "They knew Kureishi . . . had carved a lucrative career out of his willingness to shock and that his trademark was a merciless eye on the hypocrisies of racism. But nothing had prepared them for the libidinous exploits of Karim Amir . . . who stars in the BBC drama." Despite a general reluctance to screen the show on American television, it is available to buy on video and was screened in its entirety at the San Francisco Gay and Lesbian Film Festival. America's Canadian neighbors bought the show, prompting Greg Quill in the

Toronto Star to enthuse "Rarely in television have we had the chance to absorb a piece of original entertainment as complex, as wry and satirical, as beautifully executed, as good-natured as . . . *The Buddha of Suburbia*." I'll let him have the final word to those readers who have yet to watch the video of the novel: "Don't miss a minute. *The Buddha of Suburbia* is a rare TV event."

Further Reading and Discussion Questions

This chapter complements the previous four by providing topics/questions for discussion and suggestions for further reading. Some of these topics grow out of issues discussed earlier, especially in chapter 2. However, this list of questions/topics is by no means exhaustive and readers may wish to develop their own questions and readings in light of having read *this* book.

DISCUSSION QUESTIONS

1. How might *The Buddha of Suburbia* be compared with other "coming of age" novels? You might want to think of novels like J. D. Salinger's *The Catcher in the Rye* where the narrator has a similar adolescent voice. Is there an American "feel" to *Buddha*? Certainly, reviewers on both sides of the Atlantic seem to think so. How might you reconcile this idea with discussions of *Buddha* as a very "English" novel?

2. Research the *Bildungsroman* novel or "rites of passage" fiction (you might usefully consult Catherine Belsey's *Critical Practice*)

in order to judge the extent to which *Buddha* reflects and subverts the tenets of this particular novel form.

3. How is the novel's wryly comic and down-to-earth (sur)realism first established? Examine chapter one of the novel for ways in which voice, tone and irony are set up.

4. The 1970s was a decade of great change in movements as diverse as fashion, music, and politics. Examine the cinematic images and the dialogue that help locate the TV mini-series specifically in the 1970s. List some examples of mise-en-scene to augment your discussion of periodization.

5. "Kureishi defines, exposes and debunks suburbia in *Buddha* but there is a fond, nostalgic feeling for Seventie's suburbs too." Do you agree?

6. Kureishi is interested in different types of family and in demolishing the myth of the traditional nuclear family. How are issues of family and community played out in the novel? Which types of family or community appeal to you and why? Why do you think there was a great deal of interest in communes and communal ways of living in the late 1970s and early 1980s?

7. In what ways is Hanif Kureishi a political writer? You might want to re-read his comments in the interview in Chapter 1, and look at what he has to say in his essay "The Rainbow Sign."

8. Karim is accused by different characters of evading responsibility, and often acting without fully contemplating the consequences of his actions. Do you agree with such assertions and can you think of some specific examples? Is he just naïve and unreliable?

9. What is the function of Karim's voyeurism in the novel?

10. Would you agree that *Buddha* is a "condition of England" novel? What does it tell us about contemporary Britain as we

enter a new century? Are the points/comments/assertions Kureishi makes still relevant to our understanding of British culture? You might want to read Orwell's essay, "England Your England" and his book *Road to Wigan Pier* and look at Kureishi's essay, "Bradford." Have things changed much since Orwell's time?

11. What are the implications of Kureishi's novel for better understanding contemporary British society and politics?

12. Do you think that Gurinder Chadha's idea that "having a British identity is not as important as having a cultural identity" applies to any of the characters in the novel? Why does it take Karim so long to acknowledge his "Indian past" and what lessons, if any, do you think he learns about his identity? You might want to compare him with Jamila and with his brother, Allie.

13. Reviewers seem to overlook Anwar and Jeeta. Why do you think this might be the case? Are reviewers apprehensive of confronting the representation of this family and its place in Britain? Or is there still difficulty in discussing issues such as patriarchy in Asian families and arranged marriages? What are your views and opinions? How successfully does Kureishi play such issues out?

FURTHER READING

Interviews and Websites

Kureishi is the subject of many interviews. In addition to the interview in chapter one (a shorter version of which will appear in Sharon Monteith, Jenny Newman and Pat Wheeler, eds. *Contemporary British Fiction: An Introduction Through Interview*, [London: Arnold, 2002]) and those cited in this book, readers might be interested in his scattered interview comments in Bart Moore-Gilbert's *Hanif Kureishi* (Manchester: MUP, 2001), and Kenneth Kaleta's *Hanif Kureishi: Postcolonial Storyteller* (Austin: University of Texas Press, 1998) which is more accurately a literary biography. For his comments on London readers are advised to read his interview with Colin McCabe in *Critical Quarterly*, 41: 3 (1999); and on race to see his scattered comments in Marcia Pally, "Kureishi like a Fox," *Film Comment*, 22:5 (1986). Readers may also download transcripts of Kureishi's radio interviews at <*www.bbc.co.uk/arts*> and are advised to visit <*www.indiewire.com/interviews*> for comments on his films. Kureishi also has his own website at <*www.hanifkureishi. com/*> which contains unpublished material, material that is difficult to track down, essays, a timeline, and a brief biography complete with links to online bookstores. In fact, this site is highly recommended because it is the place he sometimes tests ideas before they become available for public consumption in traditional print format.

Selected Bibliography

Works by Hanif Kureishi

My Beautiful Laundrette and Other Writings. London, Faber and Faber, [1986] 1996.
Sammy and Rosie Get Laid. London: Faber and Faber, 1988.
The Buddha of Suburbia. London: Faber and Faber, 1990.
Outskirts and Other Plays. London: Faber and Faber, 1992.
The Black Album. London: Faber and Faber, 1995.
Love in a Blue Time. London: Faber and Faber, 1997.
Intimacy. London: Faber and Faber, 1998.
Sleep With Me. London: Faber and Faber, 1999.
Midnight All Day. London: Faber and Faber, 1999.
Gabriel's Gift. London: Faber and Faber, 2001.
"The Buddha of Suburbia." *Harper's* 274:16, 1987.

"Dirty Washing." *Time Out*, November 14–20, 1985.

"Finishing the Job." *My Beautiful Laundrette.*

"The Rainbow Sign." *My Beautiful Laundrette.*

"Bradford." *My Beautiful Laundrette.*

"England, bloody England." *Guardian*, January 22, 1988.

"Some Time with Stephen: A Diary." *Sammy and Rosie Get Laid.*

"Sex and Secularity." Unpublished essay.

Selected Criticism

Anthias, Floya and Nira Yuval-Davis, *Racialised Boundaries: Race, Nation, Gender, Colour and Class and the Anti-Racist Struggle.* London: Routledge, 1992.

Anwar, Farrah. "Is there a sodomite in the house?" *Guardian.* 7 August 1992.

Appelo, Tim. "Radical Cheek." *Entertainment Weekly.* 4 May 1990.

Appiah, Anthony. "Identity Crisis." *New York Times.* 17 September 1990.

Auty, Martin and Nick Roddick eds *British Cinema Now.* London: BFI, 1985.

Bailey, Paul. "Free spirits and free love in the swinging Seventies." *Sunday Times.* 15 April 1990.

Bamigboye, Baz. "Beeb Cold Shoulders Buddha's Sex Scene." *Daily Mail.* 24 January 1992.

Berry, Neil. "Review of *The Buddha of Suburbia*." *London Review of Books.* 1990.

Bhabha, Homi. *The Location of Culture.* London: Routledge, 1994.

Boase, Tessa. "Embarrassed by The Buddha." *Daily Telegraph.* 25 November 1993.

Buruma, Ian. "The Buddha of Suburbia." *New Republic.* 203:8–9, 20 August 1990.

Carter, Angela. "A Candide in Bromley." *Guardian.* 29 March 1990.

Chadha, Gurinder. *Monthly Film Bulletin.* 156: 669, October 1989.

Chambers, Iain. *Popular Culture: The Metropolitan Experience.* London: Routledge, 1986.

Cuddon, J. A. and Preston C. E. *Penguin Dictionary of Literary Terms and Literary* Theory. London: Penguin, 2000.

Dhillon-Kashyap, Perminder. "Locating the Asian Experience." *Screen: The Last "Special Issue" on Race.* 29: 4, 1988.

Eder, Richard. "E Pluribus England: *The Buddha of Suburbia* by Hanif Kureishi." *Los Angeles Times.* 3 June 1990.

"England: Recommended Reading". Institute for Study Abroad 2000 at *http://www.isabutler.org/programs/england/recommnd reading.html*

Epstein, Robert. "Not-So-Stuffy London." *Courier Journal.* 21 July 1990.

Feinberg, Larry. "A Left-wing Look at Life in Swinging London." *Toronto Star.* 16 June 1990.

Frears, Stephen. *Empire.* September 1993.

Gardner, Geoff. "Nature of Keeping Awake: Hanif Kureishi and Collaborative Film-Making" at *http://www.sensesofcinema.com.*

Garner, Lesley. "Happy Hotbeds of Suburban Insurrection." *Daily Telegraph.* 4 April 1990.

Gilroy, Paul. "You can't fool the youths . . . race and class formation in the 1980s." *Race and Class: Britain 81: Rebellion and Repression.* 23: 2/3, (1981/82).

———. *There Ain't No Black in the Union Jack.* London: Routledge, 1992.

———. *The Black Atlantic.* London: Verso, 1993.

Giroux, A. Henry. "Living Dangerously: Identity Politics and the New Cultural Racism: Towards A Critical Pedagogy of Representation." *Cultural Studies.* 7: 1, January 1993.

Givanni, June. "In Circulation: Black Films in Britain." *ICA Document 7.*

Hall, Stuart and Jacques Martin, eds. *New Times: The Changing Face of Politics in the 1990s.* London: Verso, 1990.

"Hanif Kureishi Interview" at *http://mural.uv.es/dadelmo/interview.*

Hanson, Eric. "London Bridge: East Meets West in the World of Writer Hanif Kureishi." *Star Tribune.* 21 September 2001.

Hashmi, Alamgir. "Hanif Kureishi and the tradition of the novel." *Critical Survey.* 5:1, 1993.

Hellen, Nicholas. "BBC Sex Romp in Suburbs is Too Hot for US." *Evening Standard.* 17 September 1993.

Jack, Ian, ed. *Granta 65. London, the Lives of the City.* London: Granta, 1999.

Jamal, Mahmood. "Dirty Linen" in *ICA Documents 7.*

Jameson, Fredric. *The Prison-House of Language.* Princeton: Princeton University Press, 1972.

Jena, Seema. "From Victims to Survivors: The Anti-Hero and Narrative Strategy in Asian Immigrant Writing." *Wasafiri.* 17, Spring 1993.

Jimenez, Felix. "The Buddha of Suburbia." *The Nation.* 251:2, 9 July 1990.

Kaleta, Kenneth. *Hanif Kureishi: Postcolonial Storyteller.* Austin, TX: University of Texas Press, 1998.

Kakutani, Michiko. "Books of the Times." *New York Times.* 15 May 1990.

Kermode, Frank. "Voice of the Almost English." *Guardian.* 10 April 1990.

Kunstler, Howard James. *The Geography of Nowhere: The Rise and Decline of America's Man-Made Landscape.* New York: Simon and Schuster, 1993.

Lacher, Irene. "No Fear he May Offend." *Los Angeles Times.* 25 May 1990.

Lee, Hermione. "A Funny Kind of Englishman." *Independent.* 1, April 1 1990.

Light, Alison. *Forever England: Femininity, Literature and Conservatism Between the Wars.* London: Routledge, 1991.

Lord, M. G. "His Films Erupt, But His New Novel Seduces." *Newsday.* 20 May 1990.

McCabe, Colin. "Interview: Hanif Kureishi on London." *Critical Quarterly.* 41: 3, 1999.

Middlehurst, Lester. "A Full Frontal Assault: Buddha's Sex Romp Goes on as BBC Refuses to Make Cuts." *Daily Mail.* 18 November 1993.

Misrahi-Barak, Judith. "Yoga and the *Bildungsroman* in Hanif Kureishi's *The Buddha of Suburbia.*" *Commonwealth: Essays and Studies.* SP4, 1997.

Monteith, Sharon, Jenny Newman and Pat Wheeler, eds. *Contemporary British Fiction: An Introduction Through Interview.* London: Arnold, 2002.

Mukherjee, Bharati. "Is There Room at the Top?" *Washington Post.* 27 May 1990.

Orwell, George. *England Your England and Other Essays*. London: Secker and Warburg, 1954.

Pailter, Sebastian. "Cultural Pluralism and its Limits: A Legal Perspective." *Britain a Plural Society: Report of a Seminar-Discussion Paper* 3, 1990.

Paterson, Elaine. "Now and Zen." *Time Out*. 27 October–3 November 1993.

Paterson, Peter. "Magical Mysticism Tour." *Daily Mail*. 4 November 1993.

Paton, Maureen. "Sound of the Culture Clash." *Daily Express*. 4 November 1993.

Pruzan, Todd. "Review of *Gabriel's Gift*." *Washington Post*. 21 October 2001.

Quill, Greg. "The Beauties of Buddha." *Toronto Star*. 19 April 1998.

"Race in Britain" at *http://www.observer.co.uk/race*.

Reed, Kit. "All Style and Color." *St. Petersburg Times*. 29 July 1990.

"Robin Cook's chicken tikka masala speech" at *http://www.guardian.co.uk*.

Rushdie, Salman. *Imaginary Homelands: Essays and Criticism 1981–1991*. London: Granta, 1992.

———. "Angela Carter, 1940–92: A Very Good Wizard, A Very Dear Friend." *New York Times*. 8 March 1992.

———. "The Raj Revival." *Observer*. April 1984.

Rutherford, Jonathan, ed. *Identity, Community, Culture, Difference*. London: Lawrence and Wishart, 1990.

Silverstone, Roger, ed. *Visions of Suburbia*. London: Routledge, 1996.

Sivanandan, A. *A Different Hunger: Writings on Black Resistance*. London: Pluto Press, 1982.

Spivak, Gayatri. *Outside in the Teaching Machine*. Routledge: London, 1993.

Stone, Norman. "Sick Scenes From English Life" and "Through a Lens Darkly." *Sunday Times*. 10 January 1988.

Taylor, D. J. "Whatever Happened to Lucky Jim?" *Weekend Guardian*. 1 June 1991.

Taylor, D. J. *After the War: The Novel and England Since 1945*. London: Flamingo, 1994.

Todd, Richard. *Consuming Fictions: The Booker Prize and Fiction in Britain Today*. London: Bloomsbury, 1996.

Westwood, Sallie and Parminder, Bhachu. "Images and Realities: Our beliefs about Asian families are often selective, prejudiced and riddled with contradictions." *New Society.* 6 May 1988.

Williamson, Judith. "Two Kinds of Otherness: Black Film and the Avant-Garde." *Screen.* 29:4, Autumn 1988.

Wilson, Amrit. *Finding a Voice: Asian Women in Britain.* London: Virago, 1984.

Yousaf, Nahem. "Hanif Kureishi and 'The Brown Man's Burden.'" *Critical Survey.* 8:1, (1996).

Notes

1. This interview took place in June 2001 at Hanif Kureishi's home. A shorter version of this interview will appear as Nahem Yousaf and Sharon Monteith, "Hanif Kureishi" in Sharon Monteith, Jenny Newman, and Pat Wheeler, eds. *Contemporary British Fiction: An Introduction Through Interview* (London: Arnold, 2002).

2. Barbara Burford published *The Threshing Floor*, a novella about a black woman artist living in Canterbury, in 1986 and her comment is cited in Rhonda Cobham and Merle Collins, *Watchers and Seekers* (London: Women's Press, 1987).

3. Michael Neve, "Nuclear Fall-Out: Anxiety and the Family," Roy Porter and Sarah Dunant, eds. *The Age of Anxiety* (London: Virago, 1996).

4. For extracts from this speech, see "Robin Cook's chicken tikka masala speech" in the *Guardian*, 19 April 2001. Also available at *http://www.guardian.co.uk*. For coverage of recent racist attacks and the responses of British Asians to those attacks, see the *Observer's* special reports of "Race in Britain" for 25 November 2001 at *http://www.observer.co.uk*.

5. Benjamin Disraeli's *Sybil, or The Two Nations* (1845) has a strong political edge. It is also interesting to note an unusual forerunner of Kureishi's protagonist Karim: Dandy Mick, Disraeli's teenage factory worker, is renowned for wearing gorgeously colorful clothing in an effort to mark out his individuality.

6. See Kaleta, p. 189. He goes on to suggest, "His separation from his mother, on the other hand, is not something he wants, and is therefore a more traumatic experience. Karim feels cut off from his mother. To him, as his mother she should always be there, in the background, nurturing." There is no evidence for this point of view. In fact, Karim doesn't comfort his mother when she breaks down and cries at the dinner table and Margaret herself tells him that "fathers and sons come to resemble each other" and "you both left me" (105).

7. For a broader discussion of these issues, see Stuart Hall and David Held "Citizens and Citizenship" in Stuart Hall and Jacques Martin, (eds.), *New Times: The Changing Face of Politics in the 1990s* (London: Verso, 1990). Kureishi explores these issues in an early play, *Birds of Passage*, anthologized in *Outskirts*.

8. Gurinder Chadha cited in Anwar, p. 29. Mahmood Jamal goes even further arguing that Kureishi exhibits a state of mind he describes as "neo-orientalist" creating images of Asians for the white British to laugh at, "Dirty Linen" in *ICA Documents* 7, pp. 21–22.

9. Henry A. Giroux in an article on what he calls "the new cultural racism" writes about a profound "conflict over the relationship between democracy and culture, on the one hand, and identity and the politics of representation on the other" (p. 2) and consequently the need to articulate the relationships between identity and British "democracy," "Living Dangerously: Identity Politics and the New Cultural Racism: Towards A Critical Pedagogy of Representation," *Cultural Studies* 7: 1 (January 1993), pp. 1–27. See also, A. Sivanandan, *A Different Hunger: Writings on Black Resistance*, (London: Pluto Press, 1982), pp. 99–140.

10. For a discussion of the Booker prize and the kinds of novels that have been nominated, see Richard Todd, *Consuming Fictions: The Booker Prize and Fiction in Britain Today* (London: Bloomsbury, 1996).

11. See Frank Kermode, "Voice of the Almost English," *Guardian*, 10 April 1990. For further examples of literary influences on Kureishi see Tim Appelo, "Radical Cheek" in *Entertainment Weekly*, 4 May 1990, where he cites Saul Bellow's Augie March as a predecessor of Karim and suggests that Kureishi rejects British novelists such as Iris Murdoch and Anita Brookner in favor of "ethnically marginal ones. He's probably closest to the young

Philip Roth, mercilessly satirizing his own folkways, obsessively questing after sex, poised at a culture's edges ready to strike at its center. He also resembles James Baldwin," p. 40.

12. Richard Eder, "E Pluribus England: *The Buddha of Suburbia* by Hanif Kureishi," *Los Angeles Times*, 3 June 1990. Eder compares the novel with Tom Wolfe's *Bonfire of the Vanities* set in New York. He reads the latter as a cold but clever novel dealing with "a Western city pressed upon by a non-white Third World" while *Buddha* "shows us what it is like to be that Third World." It is clear that Eder's review is flawed by the generic assumption that his—and Kureishi's—readers are all versions of his own white Western self.

13. I would like to thank Alex Monsey of Kureishi's London literary agency for supplying this information.

14. Hanif Kureishi, "Sex and Secularity." I wish to thank Hanif Kureishi for permission to quote from this unpublished piece.

15. Section 28 of the Local Government Act of 1988 stated that that no local authority should intentionally promote homosexuality or publish material with the intention of promoting homosexuality.

16. When concessions were made, they usually involved sexual situations. As Kureishi tells Kaleta, "There's no point in shooting a lot of weird stuff because they're not going to put it on anyway. I'd have spent two days on the phone with some guy from the BBC calling to say that it had to be cut." The example to which Kureishi refers is the sado-maschistic sex scene between Charlie Hero and a prostitute that Karim witnesses and reports in the novel, but which he only hears off-camera in the TV adaptation. See Kaleta, p. 118.

17. Bowie's liner notes from the first UK version are available at *http://www.teenagewildlife.com/Notes/Albums/TBOS/linernotes.html*.